T0158643

RUNNING WITH THE DRAGON

RUNNING WITH THE DRAGON

HOW INDIA SHOULD DO BUSINESS WITH CHINA

Saibal Dasgupta

An imprint of Penguin Random House

PORTFOLIO

USA | Canada | UK | Ireland | Australia
New Zealand | India | South Africa | China

Portfolio is part of the Penguin Random House group of companies
whose addresses can be found at global.penguinrandomhouse.com

Published by Penguin Random House India Pvt. Ltd
7th Floor, Infinity Tower C, DLF Cyber City,
Gurgaon 122 002, Haryana, India

First published in Portfolio by Penguin Random House India 2019

10 9 8 7 6 5 4 3 2 1

ISBN 9780670091812

Typeset in Adobe Garamond Pro by Manipal Technologies Limited, Manipal
Printed at Replika Press Pvt. Ltd, India

www.penguin.co.in

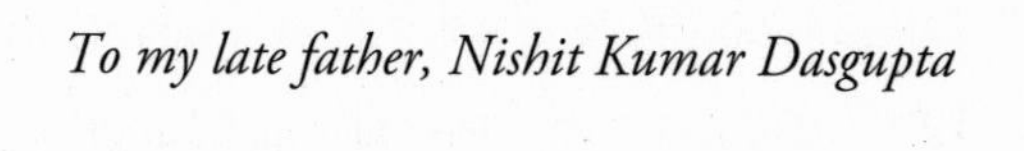
To my late father, Nishit Kumar Dasgupta

CONTENTS

Introduction ix

1. Tapping Opportunities 1
   Case study: What made NIIT a big success in China? 24
2. Aiming High: 1000-strong Chinese Firms in India 28
   Case study: The story of a Chinese consulting firm in India 43
3. Collaboration Challenges 45
   Case study: The story of Lina Shen 52
   Case study: Making business out of collaboration 54
4. Doing Business in China 58
   Case study: Story of an Indian in China's complex chemical business 76
   Case study: Business journey from India to China to Tanzania 80
   Case study: When an employee takes the profit road 82
5. Deal-making while Navigating Chinese Culture 88
6. Building Infrastructure and Influence 99
7. Trading and Slipping 123
8. Public Discourses: A Crucial Challenge 150
9. Moving towards a USD 5 Trillion Economy: Policy Learnings from China 160

10. People-to-People Linkages 179

Case study: A teacher's role in Chinese investments in India 186

Case study: Connecting musically: Indian ragas for Chinese ears 188

11. The Trump Effects 192

Conclusion: The Path Ahead 212

Notes 225

INTRODUCTION

Walking through narrow housing bylanes of Beijing, Shanghai or any Chinese city, you will find small groups of people seated around low tables playing mah-jong, the traditional tile-based strategy game. Strategy comes naturally to every Chinese. Almost everyone in China learns early in life when to speak, in what tone and, more importantly, when not to speak.

Concepts like 'killing with borrowed knife' may seem alien or extremely complicated to an Indian business executive, but they come naturally to many Chinese business executives. Past knowledge has forged into the intuitive thinking process, which the Chinese use in business negotiations almost unconsciously. Indians often talk about the great tactician Chanakya or the strategy games of Mahabharata but hardly ever test them in business life.

The Chinese invest hugely in understanding foreign cultures and markets while being confident in the knowledge that their competitors and would-be allies are unlikely to make sufficient effort to understand them.

This is one reason why Chinese manufacturers have broken into the Indian market, making brands like Xiaomi, Haier, Huawei, ZTE and Lenovo almost household names in major cities. Hardly any Indian consumer product brand with the exception of Tata Motors's Jaguar, which is still seen as a British brand, has gained a foothold in China.

Some have tried and reaped massive gains. Rajendra S. Pawar, chairman of NIIT, the Indian educational giant, told me how he spent years learning the Chinese way of doing business and gaining their confidence before the company established IT teaching facilities in nearly 100 universities and institutions in China.

China constitutes a giant opportunity for Indian companies to not just build a presence in the Middle Kingdom but also to collaborate with Chinese companies in manufacturing, research and marketing in India and other countries. Professionals looking at world markets may also consider linking themselves with Chinese firms.

What are the things they must know and do to venture boldly in this brave new world, and also to counter new competition from Chinese companies spreading their tentacles in India? This is one of the issues discussed in this book.

Most major Indian companies have either kept away from China or opted for a token presence with their offices in Chinese cities, mostly engaged in sourcing material instead of trying their hand at local collaboration, manufacturing or exporting from India. Indian government officials who have been tasked with the job of facilitating investment by Indian companies in China privately complain that many of them are extremely risk-averse when it comes to China.

The time has come for Indian companies to realize the potential of the Chinese market, find ways to participate, collaborate and think big.

There is a large untapped potential for an increase in trade and investment relationships between the two countries in different sectors, Chandrajit Banerjee, director general of the Confederation of Indian Industry, told me in an interview in New Delhi.

'Although, there has been an increase in Chinese investments recently in India, especially in the sphere of digital technology, investments in the manufacturing sectors are also needed,' he said.

Indian companies, particularly in IT and pharmaceuticals, must push for a bigger presence in China. 'Indian IT companies are reinventing their business models and can provide solutions in China under Industry 4.0, IoT and manufacturing,' Banerjee said.

This book explores opportunities for business collaboration, looks at the challenges, raises questions and seeks answers. It contains voices of over forty Indian and Chinese business executives, experts and officials who spoke in wide-ranging interviews and agreed to have their views recorded in the book.

There are nine case studies, which are inspiring stories of Indian and Chinese businesspersons engaged in remarkable work. We also look into the strengths and weaknesses of Indian companies operating in China, and the Chinese firms that have begun to unsettle sections of the Indian market.

As an Indian journalist based in China for fourteen years, I bring you a ringside view of the developments in China and its interactions with India and the rest of the world.

Are we ready to learn and seize new opportunities? This is one of the several questions that Indian business executives, professionals and administrators must ask themselves.

It is often said that Chinese companies grew in strength by stealing technology from Western firms. What is overlooked is that the Chinese kept an open mind when it came to learning from Westerners things like new ways of using technology and doing business. At the same time, they tried to localize imported technology and business systems to meet domestic needs while creating an array of facilities to implement new projects. Many of them have grown tenfold or more in their home markets, and overtaken their former partners from the United States, Europe and Japan in the world marketplace.

What drives China's global trade surplus, which was USD 351 billion in 2018, while India ended the 2018-19 financial year with a record deficit of USD 176 billion? We are dealing with a country that smashed Japan's forty-year record as the world's second-biggest economy and went on to become the biggest trader overthrowing the United States in 2012.

We should start picking up clues from Chinese business practices, something Western companies and governments have been doing for decades. We did not learn from the growth stories of Japan and South Korea, indicating a reluctance to learn from an Asian country.

An exciting aspect of the Chinese way is their tightly integrated assaults on foreign markets with several different companies and government agencies working in tandem.

Sometimes learning starts with the ability to unlearn some old ways of doing things and a close self-examination.

In the long years that I have lived in Beijing, Hong Kong and Singapore, there have been dozens of opportunities to discuss China's amazing growth story with Indian business executives, some of whom have done remarkable work in the United States and in Europe. I have heard unbridled admiration for Chinese entrepreneurs and a plethora of what they consider valid reasons to explain the tardy growth of Indian businesses.

There is no need for Indians to tear their hair over predictions by economic think tanks that China would surpass the US to become the world's biggest economy sometime between 2020 and 2030.

India is China's seventh biggest trading partner, far ahead of advanced countries like the United Kingdom. Beijing knows India, with its demographic dividend, holds a huge untapped potential that goes beyond the future growth opportunities in several countries, including Japan and South Korea.

It is time for Indian companies to start collaborating with Chinese players on a global scale. Some like L&T, TCS, NIIT, Apollo Tyres, Binani Cements and dozens of lesser-known Indian companies have dug their heels in China. The process has already begun. It is time for more players to join the party.

Political risks emerging out of events like developments in Kashmir, and ups and downs in India's relationship with China will continue to challenge investors in both countries. Some see US President Donald Trump's trade actions against China as an opportunity for India to attract some of the American investments that went the China way. In both cases, Indian companies set on high-growth trajectories are best suited to deal with the challenges and grab opportunities as they come, and not the majority that looks at GDP growth to set low targets for themselves.

1

TAPPING OPPORTUNITIES

'The Chinese "dragon" and the Indian "elephant" must not fight each other, but dance with each other. In that case, one plus one will equal not only two but also eleven.' —Chinese Foreign Minister Wang Yi, March 2018.[1]

There is every reason for Indian companies to enter new vistas by upgrading their manufacturing base, expanding e-commerce and sharing economy systems besides adopting technologies like robotics and artificial intelligence (AI) as quickly and as extensively as the Chinese have done.

In this chapter, we will explore opportunities that remain to be tapped by both Indian and Chinese companies and delve into the reasons why some companies have succeeded and others have not.

We need to wash our minds of the notion that Chinese entrepreneurs are driven purely by government policy and that they follow the directions of the ruling Communist Party even when they are venturing in other countries. Far from it. They behave independently as businessmen and -women in most cases. What the government does is provide policy guidelines—as other countries do—on the nature of overseas investments by Chinese companies.

China would not have sent out thousands of investors across dozens of countries if its government had not learnt to relax control. Neither would the country have emerged as the biggest supplier of international tourists if the government continued to watch outflows and determine who should go abroad as it did in the past.

There's a secret why Chinese companies, big and small, are flocking to India despite the substantial hurdles they face in Indian cities. Of course, India's large market is one reason.

But an important reason that I managed to get out of Chinese investors and piece together from several interviews is a kind of fear of the unknown.

'There is really nothing complex about the technology we use. Neither is it secret. It is just that we implement projects better than many countries,' one appliance-maker told me, adding, 'We are afraid Indian companies in our field would learn how to go about this business efficiently. We want to be in India to take them up as competitors if that happens and do not want to miss the bus,' he said.

It is the same set of reasons that drove American and European countries to set up factories in China and continue through thick and thin making losses for over a decade—in some cases, two decades—before they could turn out some profits. The game is about being in a place, rather than missing opportunities, to make the best of a market destined to grow.

Risk-taking

Avoiding risks in China with its image of being a difficult market is an important reason why Indian companies often avoid taking crucial decisions or look the other way when opportunities beckon them. This situation arises particularly in cases where the first initiative must come from country heads and executives posted in Shanghai, Beijing, Guangzhou or Dalian who may or may not have the ear of the head office.

What is lacking is a concern for missing opportunities. The foot-dragging demonstrated by Indian companies in the face of opportunities in China is astonishing. Chances are not limited to extending Indian business operations to China. But there is an opportunity to go global on the backs of Chinese companies that have already crafted a place for themselves in different parts of the world. If some Indian IT companies came to China purely to serve their American customers and did a good business out of it, why can't this model be replicated to reach Europe and other places in association with Chinese companies?

If you look at the top 200 Indian companies, you will find that just about a few dozen have looked at manufacturing and servicing possibilities in China. Even the best of Indian companies have focused on buying stuff and selling it in India using their label. Major Indian companies are behaving like small traders of Delhi's Karol Bagh, Crawford and Bhuleshwar Markets in Mumbai, or the scores of 'China markets' across India. I found there is one such market of Chinese goods even in remote Shillong in north-east India.

The cautious approach towards China is reflected in the extremely low investments made by Indian firms in this country. About 42 per cent of the Indian companies present in China have invested 50 million Chinese yuan (Rs 500 million) or less, according to a recent survey conducted by the Confederation of Indian Industry (CII) and Evalueserve.

A lot of importance is given to the issue of political risks. Why should I invest in a situation where the India–China relationship is hit by a storm because of border clashes or political differences every second year?

This question is asked by investors in both countries. Indian investors looking at China as a manufacturing base or even considering taking a Chinese partner in India will spend a vast amount of management time pondering over this issue.

What if my assets are seized or I get caught in a jumble of rules and regulations that I do not comprehend beyond the advice given by so-called specialists? This and the fact that margins are low in China have kept most Indian business away from the Middle Kingdom, as China is often described. At the same time, business curiosity and the nagging feeling of missing opportunities is driving many CEOs to review their approach towards China. Many of them come to China on sightseeing tours with families and associates while using the opportunity for a quick look around.

City governments in China have investor promotion departments and special agents who can arrange a factory visit and even fix a meeting with executives of local companies. This may seem very impressive until you find out that the person assigned to you is a communications executive who has little to do with the actual running of the company.

Factories in China allow visitors to their premises knowing full well that visitors are incapable and unwilling to pick up ideas in the manner the Chinese did in past decades, which also gave them the image of being a copycat industry. Chinese executives went around factories in the Western world taking pictures of machines from every possible angle and sending them back to their engineers, who then drafted suitable questions to ask for better understanding. If anything, visits to their factories can result in some sales, now or in the future.

The Chinese showed the kind of determination to learn new ways that the Japanese and South Koreans exhibited in the early and middle parts of the twentieth century. There was a time when Americans ranted against the ability of the Japanese to miniaturize anything that was done in the Western world and compete with the original holders of design and technology copyrights. The US government even tried to make laws to protect local industry, particularly in the auto sector, against what was called the Japanese business invasion. Today, the Chinese are being blamed for precisely those reasons.

This time it is different. The new beneficiaries of Western technology adaptation, the Chinese, have no fear of their knowhow being stolen by the Indians, the Russians, the Latin Americans, the Vietnamese or any of the African nationalities. Technology, at its basic level, is no secret in the Internet-driven world. What distinguishes one from the other is a human quality: the determination to excel and prosper.

Will Indian companies find in themselves the ability to think in the long term instead of craving immediate profits, and make a determined effort to learn new ways with the goal of quadrupling their existing strengths?

'For a state-owned company, political risk in Indian investment may be 80 per cent. But it is very low, maybe 10 per cent for a private company,' Li Jian, the Hindi-speaking CEO of Draphant, a company that provides business advisories to Chinese companies in India, told me while sipping coffee at Starbucks in the picturesque Lama Temple area of Beijing. 'Chinese private companies are very straightforward. Wherever there is a market, they will go and explore it,' he said.

Chinese companies are risk-takers who expect to face bottlenecks and the possibility of returning after withdrawing investments. They invest in different kinds of environments in Africa and in Latin America, taking huge risks, some of which manifest in sudden policy changes with change in governments. Many of them have not just burnt their fingers but part of their hand as countries like Myanmar, Sri Lanka, Sudan and Venezuela went through massive political changes causing domestic strife and crisis.

I strongly advocate to Indian companies, whatever their size and odds they face, to step into China. In its June 2019 report, management consultants McKinsey said, 'Chinese consumption is expected to grow by about USD 6 trillion from today through 2030.[2] This enormous sum is equivalent to the combined consumption growth expected in the US and Western Europe over the same period, double that of India, and ASEAN economies together.'

Given that China is already a USD 13 trillion economy, they are expected to touch the USD 18 trillion level by 2030.

McKinsey took into account the new challenges faced by China in the trade war initiated by the US. If this issue is resolved, it may grow faster. But most analysts believe that will not happen any time soon.

Opportunities in China

The opportunities for foreign companies, including Indian ones, are enormous. It is simply absurd for any company, even if they are manufacturing things that Chinese do better, to stay out of China. They should have a presence to learn, strategize and make the plunge in the coming months or years. The cost is not excessive if one takes into account the cost of losing opportunities.

In fact, now is possibly the best time to engage with China because many of its companies are facing a wide range of pressures, which include changes in market demand in favour of better quality, the government's insistence on environment protection and the fierce aggression launched against Chinese exports by the Trump administration in US. On top of this is the credit squeeze affecting a wide range of Chinese industry.

'This (credit crunch), combined with a potentially increased openness to foreign direct investment across several sectors being discussed in broader trade-related negotiations, could create a window of opportunity for multinationals, with scale and significance in China, and the willingness to make bold moves, to acquire domestic competitors caught in the credit squeeze,' the McKinsey report[3] said. It added, 'Ironically, just as headlines about China become less exuberant, now might be precisely the time to more purposefully step up presence and engagement.'

An important question is whether wooing China is enough to get Chinese businessmen to loosen their purse strings and persuade Beijing to encourage its businesses to look at India more generously.

Mohan Malik, professor of strategic studies at the UAE's National Defense College, thinks that the policy of wooing Chinese investment is not enough until New Delhi is prepared to bring about major changes in its own governance. 'The key reason India has failed to attract sufficient FDI is the failure of the successive governments to introduce and implement major land, labour, education and taxation reforms,' he said in an email interview. 'That is why India is unable to compete with Vietnam, Cambodia, Bangladesh, Sri Lanka or even Pakistan in attracting FDI from China. Should the "Modi restoration", like Japan's Meiji Restoration, succeed, it will lead to India's industrialization, urbanization and closer integration with the world,' said Malik, who was earlier at the Asia-Pacific Center for Security Studies in Honolulu.

In the eight years between 2005 and 2013, there were just three major investments in India, worth USD 224 million, from China. An investment revival took place during the Modi years after 2014. The emergence of India as an important power and China's realization about the depth of the Indian market were reasons for the revival.

When the Modi government took charge in 2014, there were very few Chinese investors putting money in India. That year, just USD 77 million arrived in India from Chinese cities.

India's then commerce and industry minister Piyush Goyal told Parliament in June 2019 that the country received USD 1.81 billion (around Rs 12,474 crore) foreign direct investment from China during April 2014 to March 2019.[4] He said that the maximum inflows from China went to the automobile industry (USD 876.73 million), electrical equipment (USD 152.5 million) and services sector (USD 127 million).

India's inward FDI from China			
Year	**FDI (in Rs million)**	**Grand total**	**Share in India's total FDI (%)**
2000–12	12,249.81	87,01,657.33	0.141
2013	4,170.17	12,94,824.81	0.322
2014	8,667.39	17,53,133.42	0.494
2015	54,874.52	24,51,364.78	2.239
2016	19,377.79	31,16,439.70	0.622
2017	10,693.23	28,27,679.54	0.378
2018	26,243.78	29,06,952.31	0.903
2019	3,272.5	7,66,032.02	0.427
Cumulative total	1,39,549.19	2,38,18,083.91	0.586
Cumulative total (in USD million)	**2,214.95**	**420,821.64**	0.526

Source: DIPP

Take-off point for FDI in India

The numbers of Chinese investment flows in India tell an interesting story. Real growth began in 2015, the second year of Modi's leadership, when foreign direct investment (FDI) from China jumped to Rs 54.87 billion, a huge jump compared to Rs 4.17 billion in 2013. The inflows from China was just about Rs 1 billion a year in the twelve years between 2000 and 2012, when the cumulative number came to Rs 12.24 billion.

However, the promise of 2015 has not been kept up and inflows have gradually sagged since then. Year 2018 ended with an inflow of Rs 26.24 billion, which is about half of what was achieved in 2015.[5] The decline in Chinese investments since 2016 could also be attributed to a crackdown on reckless foreign investments by some Chinese companies by the government led by President Xi Jinping, who blocked several channels of overseas outflow of money from China.

What happened in the case of Chinese investments to India is a slightly different story. Chinese companies began moving investment funds to India from their subsidiaries in Singapore and several other places instead of routing them from Mainland China. This is one reason why they did not make it to New Delhi's records.

Curiously, in 2017, when the Doklam border tussle took place, investment saw a revival, with USD 350 million crossing the Himalayas into India. The last year in Modi's first term, 2018, saw a similar amount of USD 331 million flowing in.

One reason could be Modi's own experience in attracting Chinese investments in projects in Gujarat when he was its chief minister for ten years until 2014. He visited China four times during those days and emerged as the biggest recipient of Chinese investments during his time as chief minister. Taking his relationship with Chinese government forward, Modi invited the country's president Xi Jinping to visit Ahmedabad soon after he became prime minister in 2014.[6]

One can judge what kind of businesses and markets the Chinese are interested in by looking at the pattern of their investments in India since 2005. A lot of media controversy has revolved around Chinese investments in the telecom sector. But this set of data shows that there have been just three investments amounting to USD 209 million in this sector, two of which came from Alibaba.

Alibaba has invested five times, twice into telecom, once in a consumer marketing company and twice in agriculture-related businesses.

The single biggest investment actually came into the health sector when the Shanghai-headquartered Fosun Pharma acquired approximately 74 per cent in Hyderabad-based Gland Pharma for about USD 1.09 billion.[7] Its parent company, Fosun International, has continued to invest in various sectors of the Indian economy since then. The company's portfolio arm, Delhivery Private Limited, one of the largest third-party logistics players in India, raised USD 413 million from its own equity partners as well as Softbank Vision

Fund in March 2019. The idea is to expand its network coverage for express, less-than-truckload (LTL) and fulfilment services.[8] Fosun's investment portfolio in India includes online travel operator MakeMyTrip, fintech startup Kissht and travel search venture Ixigo.

'More and more far-sighted people have come to realize that as the largest two developing countries become modernized—each with a population of more than one billion—China and India must do everything to empathize with and support each other and to avoid mutual suspicion and attrition,' Chinese Foreign Minister Wang Yi said.[9]

No one doubts the economic potential of the two countries coming closer and working on common projects in different aspects of industry, innovation and scientific development. India's highly talented professionals have been a big draw in the United States but somehow escaped attention of Chinese employers through the decades when they pushed their country towards the present status as the world's second-largest economy.

India is the second-largest shareholder of the Beijing-based Asian Infrastructure Investment Bank (AIIB) and the Shanghai-based New Developed Bank, which is led by Indian banker, K.V. Kamath. Both banks have been engaged in lending to projects across the developing world along the lines of the World Bank and Asian Development Bank. Initial fears that China would interfere and pressurize these institutions to bend to its preferences in lending to its allies has not proved correct.

The AIIB was created at China's behest to finance infrastructure in developing countries in the face of stiff resistance from the United States and other Western countries. Some of the European countries came round later and sought membership of AIIB.

The China opportunity is best understood by looking at the global role of Chinese companies. A total of 156 slots of Chinese players are listed in American stock exchanges after attracting billions of dollars' worth of savings in the Western world. Indian companies have to find ways to work with them, learn to run with them, and get a piece of the big action instead of giving up the fight before it begins. If they give up now, it will be very late to recover and re-emerge at a later stage.

Staying away

What the Prime Minister and the Minister for External Affairs say about China's potential is not fully comprehended by the different ministries which control the public sector undertakings (PSUs). The PSUs have mostly stayed away from China.

The Steel Authority of India closed its office in Beijing some five years ago after running it for several years. The steel sector has seen private firms like Essar and Jindal Steel either withdrawing their Indian executives or completely closing down operations in China.

More than a dozen Indian banks have come to China over the past decade and a half in the hope of riding the wave of the India–China trade partnership that government leaders have been talking about. Once in, they found little business barring some fees on letters of intent required in the export–import business. But the fee income was not enough to compensate for the expenses of running branches and representative offices. Besides, they had placed heavy deposits which a foreign bank is expected to come up with although it has the freedom to deploy the funds in the local financial markets. Some of the Indian banks played the inter-bank market, which helped raise enough money to meet the local expenditure. Some banks even made some real losses although smart bookkeeping can cover up a lot of gaps. In effect, only the State Bank of India and possibly ICICI turned in some profit.

Then came the orders from New Delhi to close shop. Among the banks that have closed their China operations are Canara Bank, Union Bank and Bank of India while Bank of Baroda is in the process of wrapping up its branch in Guangzhou.[10]

Why banks could not find enough market is worth looking at. One obvious reason is that Indians sell a lot less than what they buy from China. The trade balance was 60 per cent in favour of China and the rest in India's favour. China now commands 80 per cent of the bilateral trade.

One exception to the usual non-interest of PSUs towards China is the railway sector, where at least in the past two years some real headway has been made. India has started buying coaches and a wide range of railway equipment from China. A more worthwhile effort should be directed to forming some kind of knowledge and business-sharing joint venture allowing Indian companies to adopt Chinese technology in return for the huge market and business that the Indian Railways is capable of offering. Such joint ventures, if located in India, can be a base for exports to other countries. What is more, a wide range of Indian ancillary industries that live off the railway system are yet to reap any significant advantage.

A case for tapping state-run giants

One of the strange aspects of Chinese investment in India is the near absence of state-owned companies (SOEs), the mammoth giants that control the country's 'strategic industries' that includes banking, telecom, insurance, energy, steel, shipbuilding and transportation, and also compete with the private sector in areas like construction, cement manufacturing, textiles, equipment manufacturing and the exports business.

It must be understood that China's state-run giants will continue to thrive both because they hold monopoly or near-monopoly positions in their respective sectors and also because the Communist Party's control and command system will ensure they get preferential treatment.

At least eleven giant state-owned enterprises (SOEs) are listed in American markets like NASDAQ and the New York Stock Exchange. They include China Life, China Petroleum, PetroChina, China Telecom and Sinopec.

It's easy to treat the Communist Party of China as a mere ruling party with its eyes focused solely on domestic politics as you would expect from a political party in India or anywhere in the democratic world. But it's different in China, where the party controls the day-to-day lives of top government functionaries engaged in decision-making in business-related areas like industrial and export strategy, financial markets, manufacturing and nuclear and space research. This is besides the usual government tasks like military, macroeconomic management and foreign policy.

The Communist Party controls, directly and indirectly, SOEs, which run into several thousand and come in different hues from centrally managed enterprises to those managed by provincial and municipal governments.

A case in point is the Shanghai Municipality's ownership of a sovereign wealth fund, Shanghai Municipal Investment (Group), also known as Shanghai Chengtou, which has invested in a wide range of businesses that includes infrastructure and construction companies. It also has a US-based subsidiary, SMI USA, which is a multidisciplinary real-estate company with wide influence in New York City and net assets worth USD 75 billion.

This is not the kind of investment or business orientation evident among India's municipal bodies although some of them have housing construction agencies like the Delhi Development Authority under their belt. If properly developed, priced and utilized, municipal bodies in Mumbai, Bangalore and Delhi can make enormous incomes.

Even companies that appear and behave like private business are closely linked with the government and in some cases, controlled by government departments. They may include giants like Lenovo, Haier and Huawei. What is more, SOEs are linking up with private companies to take advantage of the spirit behind nimble-footed entrepreneurs, expand their influence and explore more of the international markets.

On their own, most SOEs are slack in their operations style, tend to pile up massive debt, sit over vast unused machine capacity and often reek of corruption. The government has forced some reforms and sent anti-corruption inspectors to hound the offices and homes of top executives of many SOEs. Despite these drawbacks, SOEs continue to make profits because the state-run giants operate in highly controlled markets where private and foreign businesses have no access.

India has done better in some areas like telecom, which has been opened up to private players who, like Reliance's Jio bandwagon, are disrupting the business scenario. China's telecom market is controlled by state players like China Telecom, China Unicom and China Mobile.

Tapping China's SOEs will not be easy because they are slow to take decisions and look at their guardians behind their backs for approval on each and every step. But with new signs of improvement in relations, particularly on the back of a personal rapport between Prime Minister Narendra Modi and the Chinese President, there is a strong likelihood of these companies looking for Indian partners.

All in all, it makes little sense to ignore nearly half of the Chinese industry just because it is linked to the government. The government in Beijing claimed that 98 major state-run industries have turned in the best industrial and financial performance in 2017 compared to the past five years.[11]

These companies produced a remarkable profit of USD 218 billion, an increase of 15.2 per cent in profit in 2017, more than double the rate of national economic growth.

Independent experts are not impressed. The New York-based Council on Foreign Relations reported that profits of Chinese SOEs plunged 33 per cent between 2011 and 2016, while that of the country's private-sector enterprises rose 18 per cent in the same period. On the other hand, the state sector drew 80 per cent of industrial financing made available by the government and state-owned banks.[12]

'The improvement in profitability does not mean they are more efficient or more productive, and they still aren't as profitable as private companies,' Scott Kennedy, deputy director at the Freeman Chair in China Studies at the Center for Strategic and International Studies, told me.

US President Donald Trump is particularly targeting Chinese SOEs as he demands an end to the system of subsidy and government patronage in China which is hitting American competitors in an unfair manner.

China watchers are not too worried about whether his argument is right or wrong. It's a war game, a trade war if you like, and what matters is who pulls the levers for power internationally and for what reason. For Chinese President Xi Jinping, the priority is clear: he would do nothing that would erode the influence of the Communist Party or in any manner subvert the country's one-party rule. SOEs, which employ millions of Chinese and control a sizeable part of the economy, happen to be one of the levers of the ruling party.

Why we need a different lobbying strategy

China's diplomatic missions go the extra mile—actually several miles—to lobby for individual Chinese companies in foreign countries. Companies exploring opportunities in foreign markets work closely with the country's diplomatic missions, and the two manage to align their interests for achieving a common goal, which is to enlarge China's footprint. Mission officials often get involved in business development tasks like building contacts through social intercourse and engaging in background negotiations, which can be a sensitive issue.

Indian businessmen often say they can do more if our missions conduct the kind of door-opening tasks that Chinese missions are adept at. Indian missions, including those in China, have tried to play the facilitator, regularly organizing events for presenting the Indian case and sending diplomats to visit distant provinces and cities to meet local officials and those engaged with the China Council for Promotion of International Trade.

But a lot more remains to be done.

Our lobbying effort is hamstrung with some challenges. We don't have much of a history in lobbying effort, and much of it has happened in the Modi years after 2014. We still do not have an established mechanism to handle this crucial task.

Years after interactions between business and Indian diplomatic officials, there is still some amount of communication disconnect. There's a need to work out clear parameters that determine what kind of support businesses should seek from Indian missions and consulates and what they can provide.

There have been some serious efforts by the Indian embassy in Beijing and its consulates in Shanghai and Guangzhou to facilitate interactions between Indian business and Chinese officials and companies.

'We provide the platform in terms of conferences and small group meetings. We are not a business-driven service and don't have the kind of business acumen necessary to spot business opportunities. It is for them to make the most of the platforms,' an Indian official told me. The official continued, 'At the same time, if an Indian pharmaceutical company comes to me saying it has a cancer drug with good potential in China but was facing regulatory problems, it would be easy for us to take up such a case with the local government here. The industry should not complain in vague terms, but come to us with specific problems.'

An unstated reason for insufficient interaction between the two sides is that Indian companies are concerned about spilling their beans and business secrets during discussions with officials. This is also why some Indian businessmen abroad try to avoid meeting journalists.

A close look would show Indian businesses are not clear about what it wants. There are many who complain that mission officials sit over requests and take a long time to respond. At the same time, many Indian executives find themselves restricted by their head offices about how transparent they can be in discussions.

One of their recurring requests is for speedy visa clearance for Chinese engineers and workers to be sent to their Indian facilities. Chinese equipment-makers design machines in such a manner that it is difficult for a non-Chinese to successfully erect and make it operational in a foreign country. In some cases, Chinese workers and engineers are required during the first few months or even years after a plant is installed. But it is very difficult for Indian equipment buyers to convince government officials about the need to grant visas to groups of Chinese workers. The visa allotment process takes weeks and months, resulting in work delays and opportunity losses. Visa issuers are highly concerned about the security issues involved in inviting people without sufficient background checks. There is need for a solution to this issue, which has been festering for years. China should step in to provide some sort of assurance about its citizens going to India for work related to Chinese equipment exports.

Indian Foreign Service officials are almost helpless on this count because visa issues are handled by another ministry, the Home Ministry in New Delhi. The Home Ministry has its own set of security concerns and wants to go through careful screening, resulting in delays despite regular announcements by ministers and officials about speeding up the process.

The fact is that Indian industry does not take China seriously, and generally regards it as mostly a market for sourcing cheap goods. Don't be under the impression that this sort of attitude is limited to Indian traders who supply to small commodity-traders in Indian bazaars. The malaise runs deeper. Major Indian brands in textiles, household goods and white goods like refrigerators and coolers pick up hundreds of container loads of goods which are labelled and rebranded with their logos at the point of production.

Ironically, Indian customs may be charging duty on Made-in-India goods because many of the imports from China carry names of Indian brands.

Here's how serious Indian business is about China. None of the hundreds of industry associations covering different sectors in

India have an office in China. The only significant presence from Indian industry in China is the office of the Confederation of Indian Industry (CII) in Shanghai.

If industry associations think it would not serve any purpose to have an office in China, the thinking of individual business members of these associations can be easily understood.

What is more, officials of Indian industry associations often visit China to attend conferences and fairs on the strength of free tickets and hotel rooms provided by Chinese hosts and then show it as lobbying efforts. I know the case of an Indian association that was in a quandary about the need to refuse financial support offered by the government in New Delhi when it found that Chinese hosts were picking up the tab.

The Chinese are generous hosts, and this is one reason visiting Indians admire them. What is lost in the discussion is that foreign visitors on junkets end up buying something or returning with ideas of buying that they would convey to other business associates in India. In the end, the host reaps a much higher benefit than what the guest can imagine. No wonder, small city governments across China are eager to organize events and pay for the costs of foreign visitors.

Taking advantage of a junket offer is not wrong, and the business that emanates would be to the advantage of both the host and guest. The point is whether we are learning from these sort of business practices and inviting potential Chinese customers or suppliers to India with similar offers. I at least have not heard cases of such generosity.

One of the challenges faced by Indian officials and companies who organize conferences in China is the kind of local people that form the audience. Though major companies are invited, they tend to send lower-end staff instead of senior managers who can pick up cues and influence the thinking and decision-making process of company managements.

The Chinese are sensitive about direct, personal relationships except in cases where a direct relationship has been established previously. In other cases, the invitation would be dealt with in a routine manner by one of the company's lower offices. Lesson: There is no alternative to developing personal relations in China, and sufficient effort and funds must be allocated to it.

Do we do this? Before we proceed, it must be understood that our purpose is not to find fault and blame ourselves. The goal is to look for areas where we can improve our lobbying effort.

In many events organized by Indian missions and companies, I have found that little attention is paid to Chinese needs. The Chinese get lost in an Indian crowd unless they are top government officials surrounded by fawning juniors. The food is mostly Indian, with little effort to cater to Chinese tastes, and the dinner often takes place after 7 or 8 p.m., which is far beyond the usual Chinese time of 6 p.m. I have seen Chinese people invited to Indian events munching on dry food in their cars before entering venues.

Also, most senior executives in Chinese companies don't understand English and depend on junior staff, usually recently graduated boys and girls, who can translate and convey ideas expressed in events to the seniors. But there is the fear of things getting lost in translation. This is partly because the junior staff do not understand the needs of senior management and this limits their ability to capture ideas generated in conferences.

Let's look at the love of MoUs signed during official visits by Indian ministers and during tours of CEOs of Indian companies.

'I am here because we got a request to come prepared to sign an MoU. We are not yet ready. But we got the staff to pull out an MoU we had signed with another country and hurriedly made some changes,' the chief executive officer of a Chinese company told me after signing an MoU and getting photographs taken with an Indian dignitary. Indian ministers need to return home with a handful of MoUs signed with Chinese companies as proof of the success of their visit, which must be shown to the Cabinet, the Parliament and, of course, the media. With a dozen MoUs, it is Government of India money well spent!

Indian mission officials often delay signing serious contracts, waiting for the day when a minister is visiting from New Delhi and deal-signing ceremonies can be held. This is the sort of VIP culture that the Chinese understand very well because they are as dignitary-driven as Indians. But China's business is now vast and covers more than 100 countries, leaving top officials little time to attend functions except in some rare cases where events have a political motive along with business goals.

There is no independent analysis of how many MoUs signed in the presence of India's central ministers, chief ministers and state ministers have resulted in real business. No researcher would touch this subject, knowing fully well that the actual success rate would be less than 10 per cent, which is not something worth discussing.

Being risk-averse

The biggest problem lies in the thinking of the Indian corporate sector which, barring a few examples, does not consider China as a potential market for exports.

True, China is competing with us in half of the globe. Indians are trying to sell just about the same products that the Chinese are in a range of fields such as pharmaceuticals, IT services, machine tools and agriculture commodities.

What must be understood by members in corporate boardrooms in Mumbai, Delhi and elsewhere in India is that the Chinese market requires initial investments and some persistence to crack. One must see that Indian pharmaceutical and IT companies put in massive efforts to open the US and other Western markets for themselves one or two decades ago. They haven't put in 10 per cent of that kind of effort for the world's second-largest economy.

'Our companies are bottom-line oriented. They want immediate results. That doesn't work in China where trust-building is essential,' an Indian trader-turned-industrialist told me.

An important question is how many of the top 100 Indian companies have a China strategy for the next two to five years. Only a few of them in the IT and pharmaceutical sectors have considered the need to have a medium- to long-term strategy for China. For example, Reliance Industries does not seem to have a strategy.

Another category of Indian companies plays the world's oldest business tactic of arbitrage—sourcing goods from cheap markets and selling or using them in areas where they are expensive. They include a wide range of companies regarded as manufacturers and not traders in India.

The Internet and growth of e-commerce has not really broken many of the barriers although many Indians have begun to source directly from Alibaba's Tmall and other platforms.

There are some notable exceptions. Dr. Reddy's has shown it is possible to create a niche market in China although it has official permission to sell only a few of its products. The company accounts for nearly half of pharmaceutical exports from India to China.

Fortune favours the brave

It is time for Indian companies to join the race or begin to collaborate with Chinese players on a global scale. Some companies like L&T, TCS, NIIT and Binani Cement have already begun the process of learning by collaborating with Chinese firms in a range of areas, including design-sharing and co-production. International marketing is another area of opportunity for Indian firms looking for collaboration with Chinese businesses, many of whom have established presence in several foreign companies.

I see great significance in recent forays of Chinese companies climbing the top rungs of the ladder in sunrise industries. Two of them, DJI and Saisun, figure in the list of top robotics companies in the world. Again, there is a lesson for Indian companies about the successes that can be achieved by putting together IT and engineering talent. China is also the world's biggest producer of solar power panels, an area where it is not battling to survive under aggressive trade pressure from the Trump administration.

We need to overcome the sense of awe that some Indians feel when they look at China's economic development and focus on examining how its growth strategy worked, study the role of state and city governments as financiers, and those of universities as laboratories and incubators that led to the creation of thousands of companies using high technology inputs. Our teaching institutions have few linkages with industry, barring a few projects in IIT and the IIMs.

Indian companies need to carefully examine the reason for successes as also failures of Chinese companies in areas like computer hardware, telecommunications, Internet services, infrastructure construction, machinery, cargo movement and steel to glean new ideas from their practices.

We are dealing with a country that smashed Japan's forty-year record as the world's second-largest economy in 2010 and went on to become the biggest trader overthrowing the US two years later. We should have started picking up cues from Chinese business practices, something Western companies and governments have been doing for a long time. It is either our media-fed national ego or a steadfast refusal to learn from another Asian country that has been in the way. The fact is we did not learn from Japan and South Korea's growth and remained rooted to our touching faith in the supremacy of the West.

The next time you hear that Indian businesses are pragmatic and open-minded, think again. I would say they are not even opportunistic or profit-oriented enough to see the rising opportunities from the other side of the Himalayas.

We need to look at China with clear eyes at this time when the Asian giant is evolving and changing its production methods while trying to buy out companies in the US, Europe and even in India. We need to watch business practices applied by Chinese businessmen in their own country and in foreign locations. There are lessons to be learnt about how they captured market space held by people of different nationalities, including Indians, across the globe.

Opportunities for meeting and negotiation with the Chinese will occur if you are doing business in Africa or in Europe and even in India. The point is how Indian players look at them, as adversaries that must be fought or as potential collaborators. Each Indian business will need to work out its own distinct strategy.

There are limitations in learning from China not just because it is under a different political system and is very different in a dozen other ways, but also because of its government's reluctance to open up to foreign countries, even less to India. A change of heart in Beijing, which Prime Minister Narendra Modi is hoping for, would open up the floodgates for Indian exports, which can easily rise 50–70 per cent in a few years. But that would take a lot of political collaboration and a good amount of give and take to happen.

China's growth story does not mean India will be fighting the Chinese onslaught on world markets with its back to the Himalayan wall. There are opportunities galore.

In a queer marriage between capitalism and communism, Communist officials see their role as business facilitators in patriotic terms. In football terms, an official may hold any position of the lead striker, the midfielder or the goalkeeper depending on the situation.

The circumstances are different in India and elsewhere where officials are careful to separate the government from private business, often fearing vigilance investigations if they get too close to businessmen.

Most Indian companies, including those regarded as giant manufacturers, have been busy purchasing goods from the Chinese market without making any effort to sell in China, leave aside building brands.

Recent signs of expansion and growth in the domestic market might persuade some Indian companies to stay away from international adventures, including investments in China. That would be a major mistake. Indian firms should see rising domestic gross domestic product (GDP) as an opportunity to leverage using the Indian market as a negotiation chip.

High growth for a few years cannot obliterate the fact that the total size of the Chinese GDP is three times than that of India's. What is more, China sells three times more to India than it buys, resulting in a torturous deficit for New Delhi.

We shall now look at a PricewaterhouseCoopers (PWC) report *World in 2050*, according to which India's share of world GDP will more than double from 7 per cent in 2016 to 15 per cent in 2050. China will lead with a 20 per cent share, followed by the US at 16 per cent.[13]

When it comes to Purchasing Power Parity (PPP), India will emerge to the second rank at 15 per cent of world GDP after China, which will dominate at 20 per cent. The US share will actually sink from 16 per cent to 12 per cent, taking the third position below India. Few in India would readily accept this idea of actually rising above the US in any parameter, leave aside purchasing power capability. But PPP is a complex economic theory dependent on the values of different currencies and one needs to be careful about being elated or dejected by proclamations based on the concept.

Case study: What made NIIT a big success in China?

There is much to learn from the way Rajendra Singh Pawar, a Padma Bhushan awardee, launched what has emerged as the largest Indian company in China in terms of the number of people employed.

NIIT has trained over half a million learners in various IT skills and worked with over 100 Chinese universities in its twenty-one-year presence in China. It has trained 38 million learners across forty countries since 1981. The mission is to bring people and computers together. It entered the Chinese market in 1997.

'As a rule, I go to a country for a short vacation if I plan to launch business in it. That's what I did in China in 1996,' Pawar once told me.

NIIT already had a partner with huge infrastructure capabilities, and it facilitated the company's entry into China the next year. But the partner was to exit from the education business after the Asian financial crisis in 1999, allowing NIIT to take full charge of the China business.

This is one bit of learning for Indian companies that have strong contacts with multinational corporations to facilitate their entry into China in diverse ways.

'It became very obvious to me that it was going to be useful for the Chinese society to partner with us in education and skill building,' Pawar said.

The Chinese were keen in the talent area. Soon, province after province, one local government after another saw NIIT as a valuable partner. Of course, there was a stiff learning curve and the company had to continually adjust itself to local requirements.

'We had to model and remodel our business to make sure that we are accepted and provided avenues to participate. Over the years, many different models have been tried with local governments and with universities,' he said.

Pawar said that China was too large a country for NIIT to invest the kind of money required to build a consumer brand. This is why it chose to do business with business instead of direct business to consumer interaction.

'As you know in an economy and society like China, the best way to be effective in business relations is to engage with the government,' he said.

India is a global brand in IT. China has watched India's IT growth with great curiosity. The economic value that the Indian software industry has created for the US goes into hundreds of billions of dollars. If India can add economic value to the US economy, it can certainly do the same in developing countries.

I asked Pawar why he thought many Indian IT companies have not succeeded in China.

'One of the USPs is that they love what we are offering them. We are helping them to be self-sufficient, at least in IT,' he said.

'We try to put ourselves in the shoes of the customer completely,' he added.

NIIT works in cooperation with universities, software parks and local governments across Chinese cities and provinces. It is linked to software parks in Chongqing, Qingdao, Haikou, Guiyang, Gui'An, Tongren and Ningxia.

'Our graduates are scattered around China in many companies, including IBM, China Telecom, NTT DATA, Hewlett-Packard, Bertelsmann, Bank of Shanghai, UFIDA software, TCS, Infosys, Tech Mahindra and Wipro,' said Kamal Dhuper, Country Head, NIIT China.

Job placement rate for students trained by NIIT is over 90 per cent, he said. The company jointly operates IT colleges with five universities, including Qingdao University, Ningxia University, Hainan University, Guizhou Normal University and Ningxia Normal University. The seven-semester programme is embedded in the four-year software engineering programme of these universities. Courses cover Java programming track, Dot Net programming track, Open source programming track, Big Data technologies track and courses on new technologies artificial intelligence, machine learning and NLP. Upon graduation, students can go for higher studies or opt for a job. Around 30 per cent choose to continue their studies with master's degree programmes in China and abroad. Others join the industry.

Typical jobs are programmer, software engineer, software testing, data analyst, data scientist, sales and marketing for technology products and associate IT faculty in training business and universities. Doing a master's programme as compared to undergraduate studies ensures a higher success rate.

Students who choose to do the GNIIT programme in English with the help of Indian trainers find themselves better prepared to work in global MNCs and find it easier to get admission in universities abroad. Some of the students have also got into the academic exchange programme at NIIT University in Neemrana, Rajasthan.

The big breakthrough came for the company in 2005 when the Jiangsu provincial government invited NIIT to partner with more than 50 universities and colleges to train 50,000 people with IT and English language skills in the province. By 2016, it had trained double the number of students originally envisaged.

The governments in Wuxi, Chongqing, Suzhou, Changzhou, Qingdao, Haikou and Zhangjiagang have also involved NIIT to support their talent development objectives through public–private partnerships with software parks.

The provincial government of Guizhou invited NIIT to develop large-scale talent for big data analytics to meet the government's vision of positioning the province as the big-data capital of China in 2015. This led to the training of over 50,000 students. The Ningxia provincial government also tasked NIIT to use the public–private partnership model through two projects to develop talent to operate a training base in a software park in the city of Yinchuan and work with universities in the province.

The NIIT curricula and pedagogy is embedded in a four-year bachelor's degree programme that has been taught by the NIIT faculty since 2017. It works with local and multi-national enterprises in China to provide end-to-end solutions for sourcing, training and hiring of entry-level IT workforce as well as IT professionals with prior work experience.

The company has received several awards from different local governments in China. 'NIIT has helped many international and domestic companies such as IBM, China Telecom, Ford, HP, Bertelsmann, TCS, Mahindra Satyam, Infosys, Bank of Shanghai, Shanda, HiSoft, Freeborders and U Soft to source, train and hire their talent,' Dhuper said.

2

AIMING HIGH: 1000-STRONG CHINESE FIRMS IN INDIA

The Chinese, among the world's largest investors, are only now getting a taste of India. This is a take-off point, the initial testing period for many Chinese multinationals who sit over a web of investments across several countries and have only now taken the India road.

Nearly 1000 small and big Chinese companies have built a presence in India. An estimated USD 20 billion has flowed into India from Chinese companies, half of them through the FDI route and the other half in the form of equity investments in existing Indian companies.

The bulk of Chinese investments have taken place during the BJP government under Prime Minister Narendra Modi since 2014. Many believe that Chinese investments will grow at a high pace, possibly 30 per cent a year or even more, now that they have started the ball rolling.

At this point, China is not yet in the list of the top ten countries investing in India. It's a poor record, admittedly, making a farce of high-sounding political commitments about the strategic and economic partnership between the Himalayan neighbours who share a common history in terms of early Buddhism and as two Asian countries having similarities in culture.

India is younger than China by an average age of eight years. This in itself is a sufficient reason for Chinese businesses to be drawn towards India as a younger population is not just filled with energy but is also exposed to modern thinking and use of newer technologies.

By 2020, the average age in India is expected to be twenty-nine years while that in China will be thirty-seven and the average in Japan forty-eight. In other words, India is about eight years younger than China. The Middle Kingdom dramatically reduced childbirth with its three-decade-long one-child policy. In fact, one reason why China is intensifying the use of robotics and other systems of high automation is its fear of severe labour shortages, which has already begun to show up.

It is therefore clear that China has much to gain by investing in India, which offers a young labour force and growing consumer base.

Prime Minister Narendra Modi has set a target of nearly doubling India's economy from USD 2.7 trillion by March 2019 to USD 5 trillion in 2024. That would mean doubling the rate of growth—7 per cent of GDP—which may seem like a tall order. But ambitions are necessary, and one would expect the Modi government's second term to strive as intensely as it can.

The Chinese are late entrants to India compared to American, European and some Japanese and South Korean companies who came in in the 1990s and 2000s, when market access was tough both because of political reasons and lobbying by a section of the domestic industry that was afraid of competition. But they have started coming in significant numbers from 2014 onwards, and seem to be determined to use India as not just another investment destination but also a location that offers a massive market available for tapping.

The Chinese are already pushing away Western and Indian competitors from areas they want to occupy. Their zeal, determination and deep pockets make analysts believe that China will soon become one of the top 10 sources of FDI in India and quickly rise up in that ladder to take the fifth or sixth slot.

A look at the extent and nature of Chinese investments in India is revealing. Speaking in Parliament in June 2019, commerce and industry minister Piyush Goyal said that the country received USD 1.81 billion (around Rs 12,474 crore) as FDI from China between April 2014 and March 2019.[1]

He then went on to list the sectors which received the maximum amount of investment; these were the automobile industry (USD 876.73 million), electrical equipment (USD 152.5 million) and the services sector (USD 127 million).

During the same five-year period ending March 2019, India received FDI worth USD 13.62 billion from the US. Sectors that US investors preferred were computer software, hardware, automobile industry and the services sector, the minister said.

There is a problem with the numbers concerning Chinese investments as the Indian government takes into account only funds that flow out of Mainland China. But the fact is that the Chinese companies send out huge sums of money from their offices in the US, Singapore and Hong Kong. These investments are accounted for separately in New Delhi.

'I think actual investments by all Chinese companies put together would be of the order of USD 9 billion or more in the past five years,' a government official, who preferred to be anonymous, told me in an interview.

But Chinese participation in the Indian market is still meagre compared to the overall potential if you considered the need and capability of Chinese business to invest and the vast size of the Indian market. Analysts say that not even the surface has been scratched and the sky is the limit.

'Five years ago, if someone had asked me if Chinese companies face a perception issue in penetrating the Indian market, I would have said they do—it was a real problem in both business-to-business and business-to-consumer markets. Today that has changed,' Santosh Pai, partner, Link Legal Indian Law Services, told me in an interview.

The impression about the supposed risks and unreliability of the Indian market has not yet vanished from the Chinese corporate mind, but it has undoubtedly lessened after Chinese mobile and other companies have made an impressive dent among Indian customers.

'Chinese companies realize the Indian market is too big to ignore. Just being big in India can change the fortunes of a Chinese company,' says Pai. He believes they have crossed the tipping point in terms of perception about India.

Lei Jun, the founder of smartphone company Xiaomi, recently explained why India is now attractive.

'Regarding US-China tensions, it is getting difficult for Chinese companies to invest in the US. We are most active in investing in India, and it will also be good for this country. Yes, investments will grow in India due to what is happening between the US and China,' he told the *Economic Times* in an interview.[2] 'There are currently not many Chinese companies doing business in India, and we have a lot of room to improve. We are bullish,' he said.

An important question is what attracts Chinese companies to India. Is it just that they have now woken up to the fact that the Indian market is vast or do they regard India as a possible base for production and exports to other parts of the world?

They have begun shifting industrial capacity, including those units hit by stringent pollution laws at home, to countries like Vietnam and, to a smaller extent, Indonesia. They consider India to be a good location for this purpose because it offers both a huge market and the possibility of exports elsewhere.

'China has emerged as a good source for Indian start-ups facing funding difficulties,' Mohammed Saqib, Secretary-General of the India China Economic and Cultural Council told me in an interview.

Chinese investments can prove to be some kind of a 'learning curve' for smaller Indian companies in terms of leveraging different aspects of the market. The Chinese model of managing markets could be easier to absorb for Indian firms than those evolved in the US, he further said.

The nature of Chinese investments in India is worth looking at closely. A lot of money, perhaps the major part of Chinese FDI, has flown into Internet-related businesses in India. The businesses include Alibaba investing USD 500 million in Snapdeal and another USD 700 million in Paytm around 2015. Tencent, China's biggest Internet company, followed the next year, investing USD 150 million in Hike, a messaging app. A group of Chinese poured USD 900 for media.net.

The enthusiasm picked up momentum with Alibaba and Tencent announcing deals worth USD 2 billion in 2017. They include a second tranche of Alibaba's investments worth USD 177 million in Paytm, USD 150 million in Zomato, USD 100 million in FirstCry and USD 200 million in Big Basket. Tencent poured USD 400 million in Ola, USD 700 million in Flipkart and went in for the second round of investment in Practo. The following year, 2018, China's drug giant Fosun Pharma swung into action, making the first acquisition of an Indian drug maker, Gland Pharma, for USD 1.09 billion.

The World's Economic Forum ranked China twenty-seventh in its Global Competitiveness Report for 2017–18 while putting India in the fortieth place. But news of the Indian economy growing a little faster than China's caused a lot of eyes to turn towards India.

Though Chinese presence in mobile phones is most noticed, they have really spanned out to a wide area of Indian business that includes real estate, electronics, renewable energy, textiles and automotive and financial investments in start-ups.

Betting on India

China's markets are reaching saturation point, leaving Chinese companies with no option other than looking for new markets. Besides, the constant technology upgradation in China is adding to the costs of local companies already harassed by rising land and labour costs. Hence, the market drive to new areas like Vietnam, Indonesia, Malaysia and India.

Stakes are high and foreign companies are excited about India. Estimates drawn up by investment bank Morgan Stanley show that India's e-commerce market will grow at a 30 per cent compound annual growth rate for gross merchandise value to be worth USD 200 billion by 2026.[3] This is a thirteen-fold growth in the e-commerce market in 2026 from USD 15 billion in 2016. Digital payments by Indians are expected to climb from 8 per cent of personal expenditures in 2017 to 36 per cent in 2027.[4]

India can be a big profit-making destination for foreign countries which persevere in the face of several hurdles and staying power. Haier, an early entrant in consumer durables, starting in 2007 with sales of USD 42 million, is now hoping to rake up sales of USD 1 billion—more than a twenty-fold jump—by 2020. It has been trying to localize its product offerings to be efficient in terms of the time-to-market and obtain cost advantage by way of tax and transportation savings and low-cost labour. Qingdao-based Haier has used the past years to raise sales more than five-fold from USD 42 million in 2007 to 250 million in 2016.

Another company that has set a sales target of USD 1 billion is SANY, the giant construction machinery-maker.

India has suddenly become so important that companies from China are now competing with each other as they do in their home market. Besides the mobile phone business, which has several Chinese brands, the other such competitive sector is construction equipment manufacturing. Chinese firms Sany, Liugong, Zoomlion and XCMG are locked in the race for bigger market share. Again, the electrical equipment segment has three players from the Middle Kingdom—Tebian Electric Apparatus (TBEA), Baoding Tianwei Baodian (TWBB), and Highly Electrical. All of them have manufacturing bases in Gujarat.

Chinese love to go to places where other Chinese have gone and done well. This cluster approach learnt at home has influenced the location of Chinese manufacturing units to a few specific areas. Most Chinese investments have gone to Andhra Pradesh (Sri City,

Visakhapatnam), Telangana (Hyderabad), Maharashtra (Pune, Chakan, Ranjangaon), Gujarat (Vadodara, Sanand), Karnataka (Bengaluru), Uttar Pradesh (Noida, Greater Noida), and Haryana (Bawal, Manesar).

In recent years, Chinese investors have considered several locations in less-developed Indian states for basing their industries but later discarded them.

Governments in other states should ask themselves why they failed to attract investments from China although chief ministers of almost all Indian states have held roadshows and made speeches in Chinese cities in recent years. Two reasons stand out: they are unable to follow up on promises made during road shows—they made empty promises that could not stand simple checks by researchers—and they were unable to satisfy queries of Chinese investors. Some states promised to provide large tracts of land for Chinese companies around major cities like Indore or Raipur but it was later found that so much land was not available in one place or plot.

In fact, one of the biggest challenges faced by investors of all foreign countries is the non-availability of land without going through years of waiting and court litigation. Though state governments promise to acquire the land for industrial use and take on themselves the responsibility of land allotment, the reality is very different. Farmers whose lands are acquired or whose lands are slated for acquisition easily obtain court intervention and get the process blocked. State-level leaders, who depend on local popularity, can hardly risk public ire.

Feeding the PM's Make in India dream

Analysts believe that investors from China have intelligently synchronized the government's Make in India programme with their investments. This is what they do in the case of the domestic industry as everyone abides by the government line because it fits the investors' long-term goals. The Chinese do not align their investments because of the fear of the authorities, as the Western media would have us believe. It is part of the centuries-old Confucian culture in China to abide by the authorities, who are regarded as parents and guardians.

As with any international investors, Chinese investors also look at tax-saving opportunities to decide not just the destination of investment but also the source from which the money will flow. This is why some Chinese FDI has come from Chinese subsidiaries in countries that have favourable bilateral tax treaties in India and why the actual Chinese FDI is more than double of what the government has on its record.

In the automobile sector, Chinese companies are rushing in to take their place along with Indian companies such as Tata, Mahindra & Mahindra and Ashok Leyland; Japanese brands such as Maruti-Suzuki, Honda and Toyota; and the South Korean brand Hyundai. Even though there are several international companies in India and the auto sector is going through some bad days, the fact remains that the country offers a market with huge potential in areas like electric vehicles, buses, trucks and passenger cars. But Chinese companies face the uphill task of competing against reliable supply chains and distribution networks by entrenched players.

China's SAIC Motor Corp and BYD Auto Co Ltd have made their entry and plan to expand. Another company, Wanfeng Autowheel, invested about USD 50 million in a factory at Bawal, Haryana, in 2013. Wanfeng has a significant share of the market for two-wheeler alloy wheels, supplying to customers which include Hero, Honda, Bajaj and TVS. It produces three million units of aluminium wheels per annum.

It is good news for many Chinese companies like BYD that the Indian government has decided to almost force a section of the automobile industry to produce and sell electric vehicles as a means to fight air pollution. China is a big player in this sector and is expected to outdo long-entrenched companies who chose models and production schedules looking at the prices of diesel and petroleum.

Another reason why Chinese should celebrate—instead of complaining about market access problems in India as some do—is that the government is opening up vast opportunities for the export of China-made batteries and encouraging battery makers to produce in India. China is the biggest manufacturer of batteries.

'In the solar sector, Chinese companies command 90 per cent market share in India,' said Divya Pranav, senior assistant vice president at Invest India, which is backed by the Federation of Indian Chambers of Commerce and Industry.

Companies like Trina Solar, JA Solar and Jinko, Yingli, Hareon are big players. CETC and Longi bought land at Sri City, Andhra Pradesh, to setup first Chinese solar module manufacturing facilities last year.

With Haier leading the way for Chinese companies, they are making a presence in consumer durables, which has been largely dominated by South Korean firms LG and Samsung and followed by Indian and Japanese majors such as Videocon and Panasonic. There are other important players like Godrej Appliances, Blue Star, and the Tata-owned Voltas.

China, which plans to build infrastructure projects across the world, also needs to feed its businesses engaged in making construction machinery and undertake major building projects overseas. Sensing opportunity, crane- and other equipment-maker SANY established a factory at Chakan, Pune, to manufacture excavators, cranes and concrete pumping machines. The company, which has also stepped into wind energy, plans to invest a total of USD 2 billion.

Indian Railways have been considering buying Chinese equipment because they are much less expensive than those made in the Western world. But going whole hog for Chinese buying would have raised political hackles two years ago and the Railways have been conservative in their orders. Still, the CRRC has won seven orders for supplying metro coaches and components to Kolkata, Noida and Nagpur. It has been engaged in a joint venture with Pioneer (India) Electric to assemble electric motors at a factory at the industrial township of Bawal in Haryana, built at a cost of USD 63.4 million.

Chinese developers Dalian Wanda Group and China Fortune Land Development caused a stir in India when they promised to invest several billion dollars on property development in Haryana and elsewhere in 2015. These companies stepped forward during confidence-generating meetings between Prime Minister Narendra Modi and Chinese President Xi Jinping in 2014.

The planned projects fell through both because the projects were not conceptualized considering local conditions in the politically charged field of land acquisition in India and because the owners of these companies had their own difficulties.

Chinese brands on the lips of Indian consumers

Several Chinese brands like Haier, Huawei, Xiaomi, Lenovo and ZTE are now household names in India. Let's look at some of the major Chinese companies that have made a big mark in India.

Haier Appliances India Ltd, the Indian version of China's Haier, has established itself as one of the leaders in the white goods market after buying out GE's Whirlpool brand, which came with an extensive network of distributors. It is now selling premium washing machines and other goods under the GE brand and medium-priced goods under its own brand. Entering India in 2004, Haier expanded to offer the Indian consumer a range of home appliances like television, refrigerators, air conditioners, smart phones and washing machines.

Jiangsu Overseas Group Companies (JOC) is a mainly state-owned trading firm which has an office in Delhi since 1998. It is trying to push Chinese exports to India. It is trying to sell China-made industrial plants, chemicals, metals, red earth, consumer electronics and medical equipment in India.

Huawei is doing very well in the Indian market even though it is currently caught in the middle of serious trade differences between

China and the US. The Indian government has invited it to conduct 5G trails, which means it may be the first company to introduce the new technology in India. It also offers equipment for communication, and network resolutions to data and optical communications and mobile and fixed communications.

FiberHome Technologies Group is one of the few companies mentioned by the Embassy of the People's Republic of China in India in its website. The Group has served the optical fibre needs of GAIL, PGCIL, RailTel, MTNL in India, the website states.

China Shougang International Trade & Engineering Corp. (CSITEC) has supplied Bar Mill, Welding Pipe Plant, Steel Making Shop and contracted modernization of Blast Furnace for Indian customers, including SAIL, Jindal, Essar and Ispat. In turn, it is bringing metallurgical coke, other metallic auxiliary materials and refractory products from China to India.

ICSGC is a major Chinese importer, which has a liaison office in India to despatch large quantities of iron ore to China.

Lenovo, the Chinese computer and laptop maker, is now competing with other foreign brands like HP, Samsung and Apple to lure the Indian buyer. Its Vibe and K3 Note series of mobile phones have made a mark in India.

TCL is targeting the Indian television market. This company, headquartered in the boom city of Shenzhen in south China, also sells air conditioners, home theatres, refrigerators and telephones.

Xiaomi, which offers mobile phones that look like iPhones, has a fan following of its own among young consumers in India. It has perfected the art of drawing hordes of crazed customers trying to book phones online in a short period under its flash sales strategy.

ZTE is a big company in China but its mobile phones and tablets have limited recognizability in India. When it comes to sales capability, not all Chinese companies are made equal.

Gionee is another smartphone brand offering both products that have extremely low prices as well as fairly high-end pricing.

Vivo is competing with Xiaomi in the mobile phone market through a wide network of branded shops. It came to wider notice when it funded the Indian Premier League.

Oppo, one more smartphone seller from China, is also trying to attract the Indian buyer with a wide offering that includes Blu-Ray players, smartphones, headphones and amplifiers.

Significant Chinese investments

- The renewal energy sector witnessed two important investments. In 2018, CETC (China Electronics Technology Group Corporation) invested USD 50 million in Sri City, Andhra Pradesh, for a 200 megawatt (MW) solar photovoltaic cell (PVC) manufacturing facility. The production is likely to commence by December 2019. The same year saw Longi Solar Technology investing around USD 309 million is Sri City for the production of 1 gigawatt (GW) of mono-crystalline silicon cell and modules each. This solar-based factory will commence production by January 2020.
- The automotive sector was invested in by SAIC Motors, which put in USD 330 million in Halol, Gujarat in 2017. They acquired a General Motors factory spread across 170 acres with a capacity to produce 80,000 units every year. SAIC is refurbishing the plant.
- India's steel manufacturing sector was greeted by Chinese firm Tsingshan Holding Group, which rolled out big plans of investing USD 1 billion in an integrated plant in the Kutch region of Gujarat. The plant will consist of hot-rolling and cold-rolling lines as well as smelting facilities.
- Fosun Pharmaceutical has invested USD 1091.3 million in 2017 in Hyderabad, Telangana. They completed a stake purchase in Gland Pharma, an Indian pure-play generic injectable pharmaceutical manufacturer.
- In the consumer durables sector, two investors, namely the Midea Group and Haier Group, have made significant investments

in 2017. The Midea Group invested nearly USD 130 million in Pune, Maharashtra, for constructing a factory spread over 43 acres, with a manufacturing capacity of 500,000 refrigerators, 600,000 washing machines and one million water appliances products.

Haier Group invested nearly USD 600 million in Pune, Maharashtra, and Greater Noida, Uttar Pradesh. It expanded its factory in Pune to manufacture washing machines, ACs, TV panels and water heaters, and reduce dependence on imports to cater to fast-growing demand in India. It also bought land in Greater Noida for another factory in north India. The firm is eyeing a turnover of ~USD 1 billion from India by 2020.

- CNTC, in the real estate sector, invested USD 110 million in Bengaluru, Karnataka, in 2017 for the construction of a premium segment residential complex in the Yeshwantpur area of Bengaluru city. This is the first real estate project by a Chinese developer in India.
- In the electronics sector, there are two notable names, Xiaomi and Oppo, who made investments in India in 2017. Xiaomi invested in Noida, Uttar Pradesh. It started its third factory to manufacture power banks in partnership with Hi-pad Technology. Spread across 230,000 square feet, the facility will initially employ 500 staff and produce seven power banks per minute during its operational hours. Xiaomi also operates two factories with Foxconn at Sri City, Andhra Pradesh. Oppo invested USD 350 million in Greater Noida, Uttar Pradesh. It bought 110 acres of land in Greater Noida to set up a new greenfield facility. Its existing assembly unit in Noida, established in 2016, reached full capacity faster than expected.[5]

How do the Chinese view the Indian market?

It is important to know how Chinese investors view opportunities in India, and their idea of the future of India–China relations.

India was not a priority for the Chinese who first explored South East Asian countries like Vietnam and Thailand, which have 'more cultural and business ties' with China as compared to India. Language and food similarities in those countries also helped. In several respects, India is quite alien to the Chinese. Of course, there have been a few exceptions of Chinese firms who ventured into India ten to fifteen years ago.

Let's start by listening to Shaun Rien, head of consulting firm China Markets Group and author of the highly successful book *The War for China's Wallet: Profiting from the New World Order*, whom I interviewed. Shaun predicts that much of the Chinese money that will be displaced owing to the trade war with the US would flow to India. 'India is now a hot destination for Chinese companies,' he told me in an interview. The corrosive trade war between the US and China is forcing a large number of Chinese investors to look for alternative investment destinations. India is one of them. This is an opportunity to try and replace the historical tension between China and India with better economics. The success of mobile phone maker Xiaomi has got Chinese firms more interested in the Indian market. They like the huge size of the growing middle class,' he said.

Hurdles as the Chinese see them

Like most foreigners, Indians complain about market access in China. But the Chinese are equally good at complaining.

No one is justifying the stonewalling techniques applied by the bureaucracy in a wide range of government agencies with the power to hand out certificates, delay or deny them. An electrical appliances exporter who decided to turn into an investor found himself running from pillar to post to get paperwork done even after hiring local consultants and lawyers. He's not sure if his paid advisors were working in cahoots with the very officials they were hired to deal with on behalf of the customer.

Li Jian, who runs the Chinese consultancy company Draphant, says that there are problems with getting a variety of government certificates. 'My Chinese clients complain about the many difficulties they face with government agencies, particularly when it comes to getting permits and approvals,' he says. He argues that the same set of rules may apply to people coming from all countries but if there are difficulties in following certain rules, it is the Chinese firms that would be most hit because they are the ones now entering India in the biggest number at this time. 'You are given the impression that government agencies are fair to foreign investors. But as Chinese, we feel the system is unfair to us,' Li says.

One hears a wide range of complaints about market access from Indian investors in China, and some of these issues are regularly highlighted by the Indian Embassy in Beijing and its consulates in Shanghai and Guangzhou. By the same token, Indian audiences and the government need to make special efforts to understand the woes of investors if they really want a big success of the Make in India programme and contribute to Prime Minister Narendra Modi's ambition of making India a USD 5 trillion economy by 2024.

Tony Zhao, chairman of solar-equipment maker Blue Carbon Technology Inc., said things would be a lot better if Indian laws were available in Chinese translations. It would help Chinese companies come better prepared and save time and protect them from loss of business opportunities.

Chinese Internet chat groups are agog with complaints and discussions about issues relating to visas and rules made by the Indian Ministry of Home Affairs. The fact is that a wide range of documentation is required from foreign investors in China. Thankfully, the delivery of documents by government departments is quick and efficient, which eases the number of complaints.

This is one area where interconnectivity of different government agencies using common transactional websites comes into great use. An agency processing an application for notarizing documents can quickly access the database that contains details of foreigners' passport and visa for quick verification. Many of the issues affecting foreign investment in India can be resolved by using connectivity software and linking different government agencies. Will this enhance concerns about data breaches? This will depend on security systems installed in the computers and also the extent to which government can control the behaviour of its employees.

Case study: The story of a Chinese consulting firm in India

In Agra's Kendriya Hindi Sansthan, Li Jian (who has taken the Indian name Amit), on an exchange programme in 2005–06, felt that his destiny was to act as a bridge between India and China. The next year saw him joining Huawei Technologies, now one of world's biggest telecom companies looking to make a dent in the Indian market. A Hindi-knowing Chinese would be a worthwhile addition.

His experience at Huawei, which lasted until 2013, gave Amit extensive exposure to different aspects of business, including issues concerning customs duty, other taxes and security issues. The experience in the Gurgaon office of Huawei prepared him for the path he has taken, which is public advocacy for Chinese companies in India.

Entering his second avatar as the founder CEO of business advisory company Draphant (the name combines syllables from 'dragon' and 'elephant'), Li discovered there was a lot to do in terms of helping out Chinese companies confused in the Indian milieu.

'Chinese companies are facing lots of problems in India and we are trying to solve them,' he told me in an interview. 'It is about building a win-win relationship with all the stakeholders,' he said.

Chinese investors have their problems and requirements which deserve to be heard. His company's job is to find Indian ears who will listen and take their issues forward.

The task involves mapping out all your stakeholders, gauging their perceptions about a Chinese company and determining their expectations. The success comes when one is able to design the right message, communicate effectively and correct what you think are wrong perceptions.

Amit says that this work contributes towards building a harmonious relationship between the two countries, something that he prescribes for all Chinese companies in India. The work involves meeting members of Parliament, industrial associations, joining discussion groups and attending seminars organized by industry bodies, and generally making sure that Chinese interests feature in the economic narrative instead of being neglected. Communicating through the media plays a small role. It is sometimes necessary to approach regulators and government authorities with written requests, which is also what he does on behalf of his clients.

Li says that he shortens the journey for Chinese investors who would otherwise take two to three years to understand the social and business ecosystem in India and learn to deal with legal issues and taxation. Major Chinese companies get diverse management professions to support them, but they work in India for two to three years and move on. The accumulated knowledge is lost. Smaller Chinese investors do not have such luxury and need the guidance of consultants.

Li says that there are three major relationship problems between India and China—inadequate and incorrect communication, cooperation and engagement. He adds that his company is trying to find a solution to them.

He tries to resolve issues through extensive research, media communication and through community and social events. 'We want to find a way to implement the China business success story in India. But only Chinese experience won't work—the Indian *jugaad* [ingenuity] is also necessary.'

3

COLLABORATION CHALLENGES

Collaboration between companies of the two countries is still rare. There are several instances of Chinese companies like Tencent and Alibaba picking up stakes in successful technology and a few other Indian companies. But collaboration in terms of joint ventures in greenfield projects or an Indian manufacturing firm inviting a Chinese company to partner with it, in terms of equity contribution as well as new technology and global marketing capability, is difficult to find.

The best way to judge whether businesses of any two countries are comfortable with each other is to look for collaborations and joint ventures or at least attempt to create them. There are hardly any examples of successful collaborations between Indian and Chinese businesses. What we see is Chinese companies buying stakes in successful Indian firms, mostly in the technology sector, and not a real meeting of business minds. There is a problem with understanding each other's way of doing things.

Chinese find Indian manufacturing companies are behind them by ten to twenty years in not just technology but also in their world view. They are initially impressed by the enlightened thinking of Indian industrialists, but soon find that the condition of factory floors in a chemical or tool-making unit does not represent the talk of its executives.

'They are very good in conferences. They might make you feel you have something to learn from them. But they don't want to learn from anyone,' a Shanghai-based businessman who visited several Indian units looking for a possible tie-up told me.

The issue of punctuality and sometimes a *chalta hai* tendency to leave work half-done makes visiting Chinese exasperated. 'I visited the metal-cutting and welding shop in a factory. I found a lot of work had been left incomplete and the workers had been moved to some other work,' the businessman said wringing his hands.

He made a few interesting observations:

- Many Chinese companies would be happy to become a part of an existing factory because they would not have to acquire new land or build a factory shed. The task of dealing with government agencies can be left to the more experienced Indian partner.
- But to verify the historical legacy of a potential Indian partner with regard to unpaid dues with banks, tax authorities and business partners and gauge the extent of business conflicts is not easy. Some Chinese tried to use local chartered accountants for due diligence but were not satisfied.
- The problem is not with the conditions in the factory floors, which can be improved. Even account books can be rectified because a serious Chinese investor would spend on cleaning up the legacy. The problem is with the attitude of many owners who share the Chinese greed for profit but do not have big, global dreams backed with a strong work ethic.

But the Shanghai-based businessman is not giving up hope and wants to explore more factories across India because he finds the climate more suitable to his requirement than places like Vietnam or Indonesia, which draw a lot of Chinese investors. In fact, this is the reason why he wanted to remain anonymous in this interview.

Edward Tse, author of the highly regarded book *China's Disruptors*, explained to me the four growth waves that China has gone through.

The first was the Cultural Revolution and later China's struggle to get out of the system of planned economy in the 1980s, when there was no notion of what the private sector is. The second came in early 1990s when the government encouraged a bunch of educated employees to step out and start their own businesses. Some of them proved to be extremely successful. The third wave came with the advent of the dotcom revolution around 2000, when young Chinese picked up the Internet game and the first generation of Internet entrepreneurs were born. Alibaba was among them. Other such entrepreneurs began coming to China looking for new opportunities. The fourth wave was on the backs of young people trained during the dotcom wave about ten years ago. English-educated Chinese discovered that the Internet opened up new vistas for those who did not have a business background, deep pockets or the political connections necessary to be successful in manufacturing, which was at that time the mainstay of Chinese business.

'I think entrepreneurship is going to stay because it has now become an ingrained culture for the Chinese,' Tse told me. 'China is getting into a new innovation cycle with the appearance of new technologies,' he said.

I asked if he expected some significant collaboration in technology-related businesses between India and China because Indians are good at technology and not as good at converting knowledge in business, while the Chinese were always looking for new sources of technological ideas.

'I think this kind of collaboration is going to happen,' said Tse, who is also head of a business advisory company, Gao Feng. He added, 'The Indian market has not reached the maturity of Chinese markets in terms of Internet applications. But the Indians are coming along and this is why Chinese companies are interested in investing in India.'

'There are a lot of opportunities for the Indian and the Chinese to kind of break through and make a presence in Indian markets. So that's one way of collaboration,' Tse says.

Globalization is really about how to divide work and pool together resources from different parts of the world to get maximum efficiency. One way of collaboration for Chinese companies is to work with parts of Indian business that offer considerable advantages. Indians are very strong in technical areas, in software development and engineering design. But at the same time, at this moment, the cost of the Indian engineers could be much below the cost of Chinese engineers. With technology, we can ship off a block of work to India's offshore centres. Chinese companies can reduce the cost of innovation by working with Indian engineers.

I told him about complaints from Indian IT companies that Chinese companies will buy the same solutions from the US at a higher price but wouldn't pay much attention to pitches made by them. They somehow think that Indian companies are most suitable for low-tech activities. Is there a way to get over this mindset problem?

'Yes. I think there is some perception or mindset issue when it comes to discussing the most advanced algorithm used particularly in artificial intelligence. The Americans have some of the advantage. But of course, this kind of work is being done in America by Indians who live in America and they are all over.

'I think the Indians are not that far away. The Chinese and the Indians can collaborate in the designing of new cars and innovations in smart phones, for example,' Tse said.

We began discussing the aggressive posture adopted by the Trump administration in the US against China's technology acquisition.

'I think Donald Trump is actually forcing the Chinese to look beyond America to the rest of the world. As you know, China is looking closely at Europe and other parts of the world. India is getting quite a bit of focus. I know that Indians have been looking at China for some time now. It would make a lot of sense for Chinese and Indians to get closer,' Tse said.

I asked if he thought Chinese companies are ready to buy up companies in India as they have done in Europe and elsewhere.

'Certainly, India is a market the Chinese would be looking at. But it depends on what kind of companies. I think the Chinese would be looking at companies that will serve them in a couple of areas. They would buy Indian companies that would help them to get access to the Indian market or certain capabilities from the Indians, like engineering and software capabilities. Buying these companies could be a way to get access to those capabilities. There should be an increase in interest by Chinese and Indian companies to attempt mergers and acquisitions. I think the Chinese will slowly come to realize that India can be a good place to execute projects.' Tse said.

'After all, the two people share a lot in terms of civilization. We, as a country, are keenly interested in Indian civilization. But we don't really understand what Indians are. A lot of Chinese don't have a clue where Mumbai or Bangalore is,' he added.

The role of venture capitalists

An interesting way of collaboration is investing in the growth of Indian companies at the early stage level and nurturing them to be major players instead of grabbing mature companies with 80–100 per cent stake buyouts.

In this section, we will discuss the rapidly rising role of Chinese venture investments and present a true story of how a Chinese businesswoman who believes in the India story collaborated with an Indian company. It is useful to hear this story because we need many more people like her from both sides of the Himalayas.

Much of the venture capital and angel investments have come to the Internet business, which is the fastest-growing sector and is expected to be valued at USD 250 billion by 2020. The country is experiencing fast growth in India's Internet user base, which includes one billion mobile users, more than 350 million smartphone users and nearly half a billion Internet users.

Two kinds of Chinese players are active in India's venture capital investments market—those that operate under big brand banners like Alibaba and Xiaomi, and small groups of investors who are plodding through the dust and confusion of India because they see a country at the tipping point of high-growth trajectory.

When you listen to them, you realize that India is indeed on the point of a big take-off in the business value chain and its ecosystem is increasingly attractive to Chinese investors who are driven purely by the profit motive and are not fully independent of their government's policy objectives and their own need to corner big market share in a specific sector.

After achieving significant success as a mobile brand, Xiaomi is pushing its investment arm, Shunwei Capital, to play a big role worth USD 1 billion in the Indian investment market. Reports suggest that it raised a USD 1.21 billion fund in November 2018, a big part of which would go into Indian companies. Shunwei is believed to have invested in seventeen start-ups in India, including chalo.com, which provides solutions for daily commute.[1] The site helps people navigate through the daily schedules of buses, trains and metros, and map their real-time movements across fifteen cities, including Lucknow, Bhopal, Agra, Kochi, Mathura, Jaipur and Jabalpur.

The venture capital arms of Tencent and Alibaba are in hot competition in India. They are both engaged in backing food delivery businesses of Swiggy, in which Tencent has poured money, and Zomato, in which Alibaba has invested.

Alibaba, which entered the Indian investment scene ahead of most other Chinese businesses, is believed to have taken a piece of the action in nearly fifty Indian companies. The Jack Ma-led company, which invested heavily in online grocery store Big Basket, e-commerce logistics firm XpressBees and payment service Paytm, is known for opting for companies that offer high-levels of user engagement.

This may seem to be a natural progression for a company that is primarily an e-commerce giant which generates and holds vast quantities of user data. Some even suspect that Alibaba's goal is to capture as much data as possible before the Indian market explodes on the international scene as a much bigger player.

Tencent has made a wide range of investments and acquisitions in India. It led a USD 1.1 billion financing round for the Indian ride-hailing company Ola, which has an e-wallet named Ola Money. Both Flipkart and Ola Money are competitors of Paytm.

Tencent Holdings, China's largest gaming and social media firm, bought a majority stake in Indian gaming app, Dream 11, in 2018.[2]

There are signs Chinese investors are keener on the less-served tier II and tier III cities instead of sweating it out in the congested markets of tier 1 cities. The smaller venture capitalists in China and those investing in Indian venture companies are equally active. Cities like Beijing, Shanghai and Shenzhen regularly witness small and big conferences with Indian start-ups looking for funds to grow and even explore technology collaboration in some situations.

'I find Chinese investors are getting excited about the prospects of Indian start-ups. I expect a lot of involvement in the months and years ahead,' said Neeraj Tyagi, managing partner of Mumbai-based Venture Catalysts Pvt. Ltd, who was in Beijing to introduce his start-up clients to Chinese investors.

One of the start-ups seeking assistance is Playtoome, which organizes and records events of performing artists across India and shows them real-time over Internet sites.

'I am looking for Chinese funding. I have an attractive proposition because there are strong prospects for our company. We have already established a large audience base and a significant number of performing artists have joined us,' Playtoome's managing director S. Keerthivasan told me.

Case study: The story of Lina Shen

As soon as we got speaking, Lina Shen told me that her outlook towards India may be a little different from that of most other Chinese. For one thing, both she and her business-partner husband grew up in foreign countries.

There's another interesting aspect. She was introduced to a series of Bollywood movies in her childhood days in Russia at a time when Russian television used to telecast Indian movies regularly. She liked those movies.

'India has been a friendly country for me from the beginning.'

The idea of investing in India is recent. It germinated after her husband, who worked in a bank, decided to try something different along with his wife four years ago.

The couple were impressed to find India's secondary markets outperforming other markets in the world. Then came the Jio launch by Reliance Industries which made massive amounts of cheap data available in the hands of the ordinary Indian. This seemed like a great opportunity because with data availability many things are possible.

Living in China for over a decade, the couple has witnessed the boom in mobile Internet companies simply because the rise of the number of people using mobile Internet has grown phenomenally.

'We knew Jio would act as a trigger. You can see that the penetration of mobile Internet has skyrocketed in India after the Jio launch.'

The couple felt that there would be a wave of new opportunities and independent start-up companies. They began looking at possible places where they could invest. They didn't believe in investing directly into start-ups because such investments are very difficult to manage.

'We cannot filter the best deals because we are not locals and we don't understand the acquisition scene or the business culture in India,' she said.

This is when they started looking for investment managers, general partner or venture capital firms. They made a trip to India to find the right partners. In effect, they put money in investment companies that pool funds from different sources and finance a set of pre-identified start-ups. They talked to major venture capital companies like Accenture and the smaller ones before identifying what would suit them best, which is a company formed by Indian managers and with solid background in investments in India and abroad. She explained that in a company run by a limited number of partners, it is easier to easily communicate with the actual account managers dealing with investment.

How does she know whether her money is safe in India? There are always some risks. One is not sure while investing in the primary market for stocks either. But the whole thing is legitimate and that is some assurance. Besides, the same risk is shared by several other investors pouring money in the same pool, she said.

'In general, we have confidence in the current political situation in India and the mobile Internet sector in which we are investing. This is good timing because the government is doing a lot to support this business,' Shen said. They try to structure financial arrangements so that they have to take minimum risk on either tax or the money transfer. They use professional consultants.

Of course, one has to be careful in choosing which companies to support and one needs to monitor their performance. These are somewhat long-term investments and one has to wait 5–7 years to earn a decent profit, she said.

'I can tell you that there are a lot of highly professional investment managers in India although not all of them can be put in this category,' she said. 'We are quite satisfied with our partners. They give good reports and are very hands-on in monitoring companies that they are investing in.'

This kind of investing is entirely different from the headline-grabbing investments by major Chinese companies. The kind of investing Shen is doing is different from strategic investments by Alibaba and Tencent who are not only investing for returns but also to build a strategic presence in the Indian market. Strategic investors like Alibaba, Tencent and to some extent Fosun take a long-term view and consider investing across different business segments so that one venture feeds into another. They are sometimes driven by the government policy of their home countries.

But high net worth individuals who pool in resources or work along with investment companies are driven purely by the profit motive and expect returns specifically for each investment.

Shen said that more and more of the pure financial investors are now travelling to India. These are investors who take risks with the only goal of earning a good return. She said that there were very few of this kind of pure financial investors some three years ago when the couple ventured into India. They made multiple trips. What they could provide Indian start-ups is not just finance but also their contacts and accessing to resources in China.

'A lot of our business partners want to learn from China. We've done a lot of introductions for companies, and they have visited Chinese cities to meet up with business contacts,' she said, adding, 'There is a lot of interest among Chinese technology and venture capital companies in the Indian ecosystem.'

Case study: Making business out of collaboration

James Ho's love affair with India began way back in 2004 when he met a visiting Indian trader who got him interested in selling Kashmiri shawls in China. Today, he runs one of the widest networks of drug-testing facilities in hospitals across India. The story of his business journey and his insights into the India–China connection is fascinating.

James had come to India to visit his best friend, Pankaj Khanna. The two had met when Pankaj visited Dalian, a city and port in China's Liaoning Province. James had then been working in Dalian and was thinking of starting his own business.

'He suggested that I import Kashmiri shawls from India because it was his family business in his home town Amritsar,' James recalls.

James jumped at the offer and very soon he was in Delhi. He visited his friend's factory in Amritsar to see for himself how the shawls and scarves were made. This is a good business, James thought. That was his starting point, and also his first venture into business.

'My Indian friend is my guide. He guided me in the business. He taught me the business. He taught me everything about the business. I learnt business skills from him. Yeah, you know, before the business I worked for the government,' James says talking about his friend, Pankaj Khanna. In China, James had been in the Dalian city government's textile-marketing arm.

James travelled to India often for his business. He had a second idea. Sometimes his friends in China would request him to bring back a particular medicine available in India, especially cancer medicines and that too the generic ones.

Now, while James had majored in medicine in China, paediatric medicine to be specific, he had quit that line for a government job. 'I was a children's doctor. So, I knew medicine very well,' says James, CEO of Beijing Memorial Pharmaceutical Research and Development Co. Ltd.

James had been a children's doctor for two years. He saw that the pharmaceuticals industry in India was pretty strong. He started building a network of friends in India's pharmaceutical research business.

That is how a major in medicine was lured to India by Kashmiri shawls and ended up in the pharma business. Today, although James has many companies, he prefers the visiting card that reads: James Ho, President/CEO, Beijing Memorial Pharmaceutical Research and Development Co Ltd (and two other allied companies). Beijing Memorial Pharmaceutical Research focuses on the R&D business, as its name suggests.

James, who speaks in Chinese and English, introduces Indian pharmaceutical companies to their Chinese counterparts and explains how they do pilot BE trials in India and the advantages of doing so.

'In the clinical trials for generic drugs, I am not quite a great player, but I think I am famous,' says James.

James began importing more and more cancer drugs and generic drugs made in India into China. The clinical trials are already being done in China. James mentions Gefitinib, a lung-cancer drug sold by Hyderabad's Natco as Geftinat. The Indian company is now doing the clinical trials in China and expects to be able to sell it there in three to five years.

'It is the cheapest cancer drug,' says James. Lung cancer is a very common cancer in China, caused by smoking and air pollution.

There are other Indian companies such as Hetero, also from Hyderabad. Hetero is the number one in the world in anti-retroviral drugs. Dr. Reddy's Laboratories Ltd. operates through its joint venture with Rotam Group of Canada. The joint venture is widely known as Kunshan Rotam Reddy Pharmaceutical Co., Ltd. (KRRP), according to its website.

Other firms from India like Sun Pharma and Glen Pharma, which has largely been acquired by Chinese company Fosun Pharma, have branches in China. Some of them are in China to sell APIs or the active pharmaceutical ingredient while some are processing their registration and some have joint ventures with Chinese companies.

'So, many Indian pharmaceutical companies come to China. They come to China and they sell APIs, they sell some pathological transforms. They invest in joint ventures and set up the trials and sell their own drugs in different ways in China,' says James.

He sees this as the future because Indian genetic, pathological drugs are the strongest in the world. But, while James's company is organizing clinical trials in India, no Indian company has so far begun doing so in China. Clinical trials are restricted to the hospitals, of which 80–90 per cent are government-owned, making it difficult for private Indian companies to successfully access them.

China's government hospitals make good money by allowing clinical trials by pharmaceutical companies. Last year, China Food and Drug Administration (CFDA) allowed a large number of hospitals to get into clinical trials.

In China, there are 800-odd hospitals conducting clinical trials. Pharmaceutical companies have to pay a lot because their charges are very high. James says there are 2000–3000 hospitals in India that do clinical trials besides the independent clinical trial centres, which are also very important. The independent centres are very professional, and conducting clinical trials is almost an industry, he said.

James's companies do clinical trials only in India. He says that for a Chinese company to establish itself as a major clinical trial company in India, it must go through the joint venture route because local contacts and knowledge are very essential.

4

DOING BUSINESS IN CHINA

We start with a simple question: Why can't Indian companies succeed in China?

The image of India in China is that of a paradox—a culturally rich country that produces highly educated professionals even though it cannot manage its problem of poverty. The Made in India brand may be a bit of a drag for Indian companies that wish to target the retail sector, which is overcrowded by American and European brands sweating themselves against intense pressure from local brand names.

But TCS, NIIT and Infosys have done extremely well on the strength of their Indian brands partly because India is known and respected in China as a nation of IT professionals. Almost anyone you meet in China, from taxi drivers to senior professionals, will ask if you are an IT professional the moment they realize you are from India.

A good way of approaching the vexed question of how to succeed in China is examining the motivations that drive Indian companies.

Two things stand out if one analyses why so few companies are trying to make it in China despite the potential. Should they look at quick profits, which is the preserve of bargain hunters, or go beyond to establish a foothold for long-term and recurring profits?

The second and equally important question is whether we look at China for its domestic market or as an opportunity that can open up possibilities in many of the 120-odd countries where Chinese companies have explored and established themselves. It is possible to grab a piece of the big action if we begin to think big.

Establishing factories and offices in China and building a team of experienced Chinese staff could help Indian companies reach out to several other countries where Mandarin is spoken and understood such as Vietnam, Indonesia and to some extent Malaysia. China could also be a good launching pad to enter the more prosperous South Korean market.

Barring a few companies, there is hardly any Indian brand presence in China. Few Indian firms have considered it worth their while to attempt this transition from presence to brand and most others think this is higher than the Great Wall to surmount.

Creative ways can be found to get over the brand challenge as well. Indian companies looking for the retail sector may have to consider the indirect route that Tata Motors took when it introduced as a British brand Jaguar after taking over the company or they may have to find suitable Chinese partners who can lend a brand. No other Indian company has tried this example set by Tata Motors. The only exception could be Reliance Industries, who recently bought the Hamleys toy stores and continues to run its China outlets on the strength of the British brand name.

Indian IT companies like TCS and Infosys have leveraged their connection with international companies to find and expand business in China. This strategy of riding on the backs of business associates can be used by other Indian companies to obtain a foothold in China. Again, connections developed in China could form the basis of entry or expansion in the global markets. Some Indian companies like Sundaram Fasteners have shown significant growth in China and have developed their own web of relationships. The Mahindra Group is exporting vehicles from its production base in China. This is a strategy that many South Korean companies have also adopted in China.

Many more Indian companies should find ways to set foot and grow in the Middle Kingdom on the strength of connections they have made while doing business in India and other countries.

The Chinese have an unwritten system of backing each other, pooling resources and feeding on each other's capabilities when they do business in foreign countries. This is also something that deserves to be emulated by Indian companies.

Associations and chambers of business have a role to play in forging ties both among Indian companies and building connections between them and the Chinese instead of behaving as another government department with limited scope. None of the hundreds of business associations that have mushroomed in India in different industries and services are visible in China. This is barring occasions when they come to attend exhibitions—which are also shopping trips—or try to sell tents to Chinese companies in temporary exhibitions held in India. They maintain no offices in China although some of the businesses like pharmaceuticals, electrical goods and chemical industry have the financial capability to afford foreign offices and have a lot to learn from the Chinese market on a daily basis.

Clearly, the industry business is still shying away from China either because it is unable to realize the available potential or do not want to take pains even where big profits can be made.

In a recent survey conducted by CII and Evalueserve, two-thirds of the Indian companies in China said they made more EBIT (earnings before interest and tax) in 2018 than in 2017. Two-fifths of them plan to ramp up their investments in China. The survey report reveals that Indian business continued to be reluctant investors in India with just nine of them entering China between 2015 and 2018 compared to twelve in 2010–14 and seventeen in 2005–09. This is significant because the Modi years, beginning 2014, have seen a massive growth in Chinese investments in India. The report also showed the nature of Indian companies interested in Chinese presence with industrial manufacturing taking the lead.

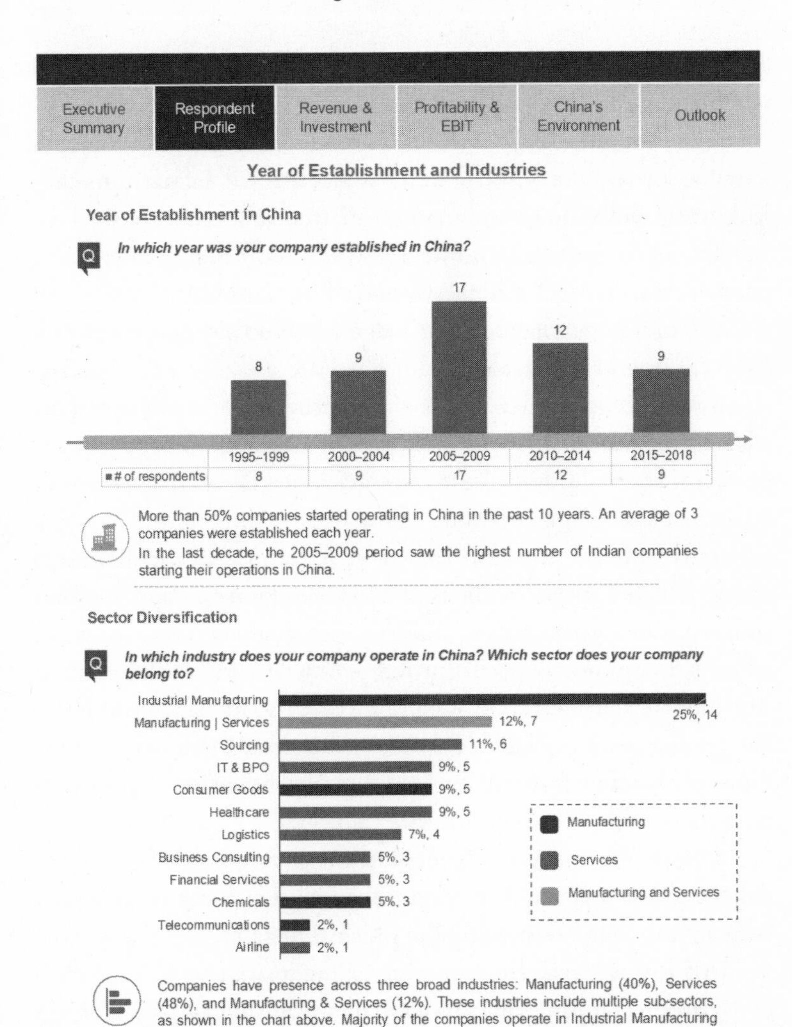

One way to build presence in China is to carefully watch the market for gaps and areas where local players may need help, and pouncing on the opportunity even before Chinese companies begin finalising deals with western firms. NIIT, the educational giant, has managed to grow year after year in China by carefully studying the country's needs and fulfilling them.

'We have our R&D team which tracks changes in technologies and develops programmes on technologies that will be relevant in the industry. Courses in China are adapted to requirements in the local market, where we regularly interact with multiple local enterprises,' Kamal Dhuper, NIIT China's Country Head, told me.

Education and healthcare are vast markets waiting for new players from China and all over the world. These are also areas where India is extremely strong. With Beijing looking at India in a friendlier manner than in the past, it is possible for Indian educational companies to offer low-cost educational programmes that can compete with the American and European competitors.

This will also provide them an opportunity for them to learn about China's special abilities in skill development and workers' training. One reason behind China's industrial success is its ability to train a continuous stream of new workers adept to the needs of the industry at a given time, something that is sorely lacking in India. Indian companies would do well to enter into collaboration with Chinese skill development businesses and reorient their poor ITI-type facilities in India with the new knowledge.

The challenges that Indian companies can face in China can be daunting and only the bravest can survive. It is a market for those who are capable of sustaining for a long time rather than those who have made their mark and money by being smart.

There is an opportunity to grow in different business sectors.

Explaining his personal perspective about the pharmaceutical sector, Madhav Sharma, head and chief representative of Confederation of Indian Industry in Greater China, told me that there are five factors worth looking into:

Indian companies should consider investing in building capabilities in areas, including understanding of rules and regulations.

In-house company regulatory and development teams need to be trained well on Chinese rules and regulations to develop a go-to China strategy.

China should be made an engine room for new drug discovery, development and manufacturing; and a bigger slice of the ballooning market should be captured, with growth and innovation faltering in other markets.

Key talents should be localized and Indian employees encouraged to learn the local language to overcome cultural barriers.

Leadership development of senior, capable, fast decision-making management to serve and support China. Speed is of the essence.

Indian pharma companies should manage China operations in China and not remotely from India. This is because the goalposts are changing too fast and if leadership is not on the ground, companies will not be able to adapt to these changes and they will lose out in the long run.

Indian pharma companies should think of setting up research and development centres in China. With a thorough understanding of genomes in India, developing that capability in China and using big data to develop new innovative generics could bring new opportunities.

Advantage China

A friend in Kolkata complains that he has no Internet for hours on end because the last-mile service provider is unable to deal with the task.

Some of the major challenges that bog down business or frighten investors in India are absent in today's China although they existed two decades ago. Infrastructure is not a challenge any more. It is not just that transport facilities are easy and fast, but several other systems like payment mechanisms and the system of obtaining government approvals are digitalized and quick. Much of the work can be done online and there is no queuing anywhere.

Another advantage is the hardworking nature of Chinese employees, who need not be pestered by their bosses to get things done in time. Excuses for not doing work in time is almost unheard of in China. I have seen representative offices of Indian companies being run by local staff while the main executive is out travelling and attending to other businesses. The staff can be trusted, by and large.

There is another advantage of being in China. Though nationalistic reasons sometimes made locally made goods attractive to Chinese customers, they are more or less open to trying foreign brands. In fact, the trust factor for Western brands is much higher than for the local ones. In food items like milk powder, beef, pork and liquor, there is a marked preference for Western brands among the better off and choosy sections of Chinese. An Indian brand may not be as welcome as an American brand but there will be enough curiosity value to attract sufficient numbers.

In any case, most Indian companies would prefer the business-to-business (B2) path because it is easier to deal with a select few bulk buyers than tussle with a vast market.

The past decades have seen Chinese companies welcoming partnership with foreign companies although several such relationships were later affected by quarrels about protection of intellectual property rights (IPR).

IPR protection is an important reason why many Indian companies are reluctant to step into China. They do not want to lose the most important asset they have by way of special knowledge of design or production process in exchange for the promise of a bright future. This is a matter of grave concern and no amount of iron-clad contracts for IPR protection is going to take away the fear that has developed after years of knowledge theft by so-called 'copycat' Chinese companies from their foreign partners.

How does one get around this problem? It is clear that Indian companies will try to make only those products that do not take away much knowledge from them. This problem resulted in many American and European companies staying away from China for years until they came in one after another, ready to surrender or share their technologies for the sake of growth in the Chinese market. They rationalized that it is better to create new knowledge with continuous investment in research and development (R&D) instead of clinging to old knowhow. They made a difficult choice and many of the Western companies earned enough to take care of the additional R&D costs. This could be a useful tip for Indian companies to consider.

Indian companies have been extremely slow in realizing the importance of having a presence in China decades after the Americans and Europeans sent business and technology teams to this country. It is already giving good dividends. A CII–Evalueserve survey showed that 30 per cent of Indian companies derived more than 10 per cent of their global revenue from China. But this is still early times and revenue sizes are small.

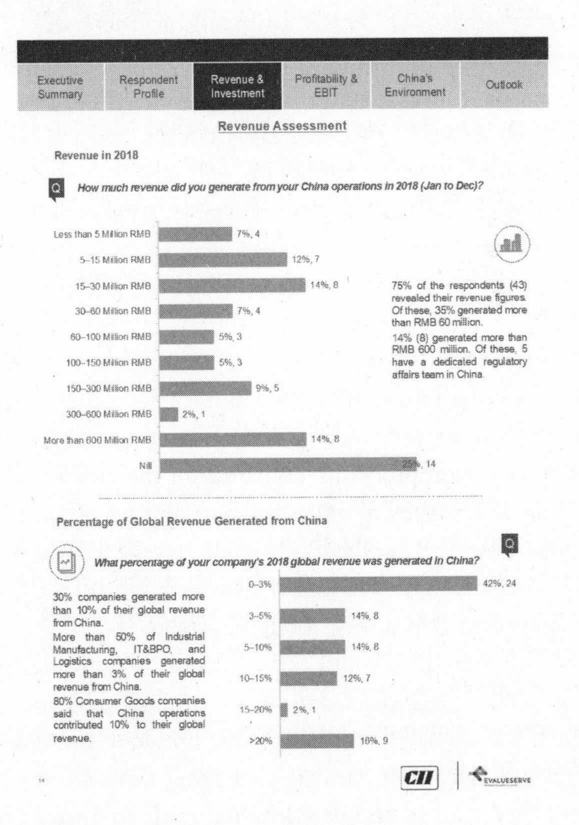

Spotting opportunities

There are hundreds of business opportunities available in China for Indian businesses if only they can see beyond their noses and plan for a two- to five-year horizon. Many of these opportunities are evident on the surface and do not require in-depth examination.

For instance, India imports 80 per cent of its requirement for medical devices that range from basic items like stethoscope and blood pressure reader to sophisticated equipment for cancer diagnostics, medical imaging, ultrasonic scans and PCR technologies. Much of the imports go from the US and China, with goods ultimately reaching physicians, government hospitals and major chains like Max, Hinduja Group, Fortis and Apollo.

It is clear that Chinese imports have developed and expanded the market by introducing new items or functions on existing goods while hundreds of Indian manufacturers have closed factories and turned into traders. As is well known, so-called Made in India goods are made in factories of Guangdong, Jiangsu, Zhejiang and other industrial provinces in China, complete with the stamping of logos of Indian companies.

Why is it that major Indian businesses have shied away from this lucrative possibility of substituting imports by resuming production, this time using high-productivity machines from China now that it is known that the market has expanded? Even with rising imports, there is enough market for locally made products as health awareness and demand grow across the vast country.

An easy answer lies in the fact that there is sometimes more profit to be made by importing and selling in India than in manufacturing. But the reasons are a lot more complex. Until the advent of GST, it was possible for a trader to get away with paying less tax than what he should and what he would pay if he manufactured the goods. There are other equally important reasons.

'The real reason is unease of doing business in India,' Mohammed Saqib, Secretary General of India China Economic and Cultural

Council, told me as we sat sipping drinks in a wood-lined Dutch bar in Beijing. He said that different government departments with their many questions, political interferences at the local level and some negative business practices have vitiated the atmosphere for small and medium industries, leading to their closure and their owners moving to trading.

If the required know-how is not available, it is just a question of tying up with Chinese companies, many of whom are eager to join hands to smoothen their path into a massive market.

India can do with Chinese manufacturers and holders of technology exactly what companies in China did with their Western counterparts in the early days of reforms and industrial growth.

How to kick off new business in China

An important question nagging many Indian investors wishing to develop business relations in China is how to enter the market and go about the task of setting up shop.

It's best to learn from those who have done this successfully.

Let's rewind to 2001 when a Marwari businessman in Kolkata read stories of China's dream successes and craved to get a taste of it. Anand Damani's family had a factory manufacturing pipes and they did some trading in India's eastern metropolis. The young man decided to venture out into the red sky of Communist China with hardly an action plan.

Unlike Marwari businessmen who rely on a network of supporting friends, family members and caste fellows, Damani decided to set out on his own. He chose the south China city of Guangzhou because it is fairly close, just 119 km from the democratically run city of Hong Kong, which is a former British colony.

'It came to my mind that if I survived six months I would make it. Otherwise, I would return,' said Damani as we sipped a cocktail of fruit juices one morning at a stall in Guangzhou. There was also some fear about stepping in a country that did not practise democracy. 'That fear is gone after living here for seventeen years,' he said.

The Damanis of Kolkata traded in silk, including China-made silk that they bought from agents. After coming to Guangzhou, the venturer began visiting factories that made silk yarn and cloth to reap the advantage of direct purchases.

Suddenly, the buying price was much lower and margins grew sufficiently enough to make him decide to settle in China.

Making his first contact was not difficult. He visited an Indian restaurant in the city, got contact details of a real estate agent and found out how to hire an English-speaking Chinese assistant.

'The staff I hired in the early days have stayed with us and have become our right and left hand in business,' says Damani.

When traders became investors

Prem Ahuja tried his hand doing business in Dubai and Singapore in the 1980s and remained unsatisfied largely because of the weather. He dealt with watches imported from Singapore.

His was introduced to China when he joined hands with another businessman dealing with Chinese watches in Ahmedabad. He started visiting Hong Kong and later Mainland China to take the business further. Every week, he visited three or four watch factories and apprised himself of the Chinese way of doing business until one day he decided that China was the place to take up residence.

As with Damani, the first person he hired proved to be an asset. He spoke good English which took care of his communication issues.

'He worked with me for eight years and gave me zero problem. I could call him in the middle of the night and he would be as patient as ever,' Ahuja told me as we ate curry at an Indian restaurant in Guangzhou.

With able staff and an alert eye for business changes, Ahuja could handle the transition as mobile phones made wristwatches redundant except for the luxury and fashion categories.

The first step into manufacturing came in 2006 when he teamed up with a friend and two Chinese businessmen from Taiwan to establish a factory that would manufacture speakers. The new business went well in the initial months when they bagged two major orders—except that they had chewed more than they could swallow and failed to deliver the full quantum of goods ordered. The order fell through and unsold inventories piled up.

Sometime later, differences crept up between two of the partners. It was one of industry's perennial problems: the salesperson, blamed for being unable to clear the inventory, hit back, saying the pricing was too high for the market to absorb. The factory finally closed in 2016 for another reason: computers with inbuilt speakers and music players were eating into the market for speakers.

By 2014, Ahuja had decided to move into a sector where technology changes would not come to bite, at least not very frequently. He entered the chemicals business with a Chinese friend who could communicate well in English. Though Ahuja spoke good Chinese, it helped to have an English-speaking associate because there are terms in chemical and other industries that are best rendered in English.

Business beginnings

The first thing to know is what kind of preparations an Indian company must make before registering and launching a business in India.

As in any country, they would need to take a call on whether they want to register a company in China or operate from elsewhere. Many foreigners, including Indians, operate out of offices in Hong Kong, using its offshore and low tax situation. English is among the official languages in Hong Kong where courts are also perceived to be freer than those in Mainland China.

A decision about where to register and locate a business would involve drawing out a China market strategy and an analysis of the situation of the industry you are engaged in. It is possible that China is the main source or market or the producer of technology for your product and being in it is beneficial.

Next you have to consider whether to be a joint venture, representative office or wholly foreign-owned enterprise (WFOE). It helps to have a consultant to evaluate options, limits and benefits before you make a decision.

'Cost and time needed for registration would depend on the type of company planned to be set up. Generally speaking, it takes one to three months to get the registration fully set up,' Sarah, founder of Beijing-based Easy Business Solutions, said.

The formalities are also different when it comes to different types of entities. 'For tax, there are complex rules in different cities and industries. It is better to consider this before setting up the operation. The company should find out about its possible tax liability before taking a decision to set up business in China because this is a cost factor,' says Sarah.

Regarding office rent, there are some cities and areas where rent is set off against tax to be paid by a foreign entity under certain conditions. This will help you choose areas where the tax is lower and rent is cheaper to save costs in the beginning. However, it is also common for a foreign company to start with a shared office with internet and furniture. This could be an interim arrangement till registration is completed.

How to build the India brand in China

Every Chinese child knows the story of Sun Wukong, the monkey king who escorted monks during their journey to India for the purpose of collecting philosophical literature. The story of the wise and mischievous monkey who fends off challenges and evil designs meant to entrap the monks as narrated in the Chinese classic *Journey to the West* has been a source of wonder and much laughter through the ages. Recent years have seen dozens of television shows and some movies made on the colourful personality of the monkey king who can grow into a giant or reduce to an extremely small size while facing adversity. Only experts can tell whether there is a resemblance to the Indian god Hanuman.

The question that should occupy us now is: What have we done to build on China's legendary connection with India to build a special image and brand for India and, by extension, Indian products? Very little.

Seen from a business point of view, very little has been done by way of building the Indian brand. Even more than government officials and major Indian companies, it is Aamir Khan and his fellow filmmakers who have penetrated deep in the Chinese brand and created a Bollywood brand. It is not so much because Bollywood is entertaining but because there is a depiction of harsh realities in most of the movies handpicked by Chinese censors, and the local audience is able to relate to it.

Indian companies that operate in China sell mostly on the strength of their own efforts but do not have the advantage of an umbrella India brand that will spell quality and reliability with Chinese consumers.

What is it that Indian companies entering China, and even those plodding along in the Chinese market, need to do to connect with the nearly one billion customers?

This is both an opportunity and a challenge for Indian companies entering China. Let's start with the good part.

The digital ecosystem has lowered the entry barrier to advertise. In times of mass media, brand-building took more spending and time. With the Internet, information gets relayed quickly and efficiently. The marketing universe in China is largely digital, with 1 billion mobile phone users and 80 per cent of them connected to the Internet.

The traditional mass media approach of advertising on TV, print and billboards does not sell many goods in China. Around 30 per cent of shopping is done online on sites like Alibaba's Taobao and JD.com. This is expected to go up to 50 per cent in the next five years as logistics improve in the smaller cities, the fourth and fifth tier urban centres. In the US, online transaction is around 14 per cent.

The time taken to identify market need, create a product to meet that need and then create the brand and monetize the returns is greatly shortened.

Some Indian companies may ask how they can build a brand from scratch as they are entirely unknown in China but have the desire to connect with local consumers as soon as possible. This is a problem that can be tackled. China has an incredible system of influencers providing a range of spokespersons and enthusiasts to create the communication for you. Food, fashion and tourism businesses make the most of digital influencers. They engage in written blogs and flow of live streaming, creating an engagement between content creator and consumer. This relationship between the so-called micro-influencer and the consumer is an intimate one and goes a long way in building brands compared to traditional advertising channels.

India Tourism, which has not bothered to further its Incredible India brand in China, can take a cue from this. Dozens of Indian tourism and hotel companies should also try to create a web campaign presence in China, which sends out the largest number of international tourists year after year. This fact is well-known to all except the Indian tourism ministry, which has not posted an Indian official in China for several years.

Kunal Sinha, a Shanghai-based expert on consumer strategy and foresight, was once advising a multinational confectionery on issues like product innovation, packaging and penetration in the Chinese market. The company was trying to determine what kind of snacks and ready-to-eat foods would potentially become popular in China.

The company was accustomed to the usual innovation cycle of twelve to eighteen months. It was surprised to find that the snacking market in China had some 90,000 different brands, many of which were very sharply localized because the local entrepreneurs knew the local tastes. If a particular snack worked, it would quickly become a blockbuster. If it didn't, the local businessman would quickly take it off the shelves within three months without suffering a setback because the product was launched in a localized manner on a sort of trial basis.

It is now possible to link production to marketing as digital platforms make it possible to gauge market demand and create products and brands to suit it. Monetization is much quicker.

'Digital platforms like Alibaba and WeChat are using a very different way of doing business from what is happening in other parts of the world,' said Sinha. 'So you are not spending too much time in R&D and pre-testing and related things that entrepreneurs have been doing for so long'.

Indian companies that have relied on the mass media approach to advertising and marketing may have to revamp their outlook. The Chinese have been brought up in a restricted media environment and the idea of mass media models creating imagery and a desire for a certain brand almost does not exist.

'You need to think of it as a digital environment and not a medium,' advises Kunal Sinha, the Shanghai-based expert on consumer strategy and foresight. In the digitized world, you are using the same platform for communication and transaction through online shopping. The communication is measurable and feedback quick. Almost every day and sometimes every hour, you learn how your advertising and brand building are impacting consumers.

Though a significant number of Indian companies have begun to sell through e-commerce platforms, many of them will be entering a new world when they find that their entire marketing and advertising focus is the cyberspace. Of course, this is happening with digital ecosystems in other parts of the world. But the Chinese are far ahead in the game. Even small entrepreneurs are adept at it.

'Indian companies need to spend a larger proportion of their marketing budgets online than they would in the US,' says Shaun Rein, managing director of China Market Research Group (CMR). Indian brands need to target younger consumers with mobile phone digital marketing campaigns. Consumers below forty-five happen to be the biggest shoppers. They also need to localize their marketing more to make their products and services relevant to the Chinese consumer,' he added.

In the US, just about half of the population uses smartphones capable of online transactions. Besides, much of the big buying is done by people in their sixties.

Chinese consumers have long memories of bad-quality products and services besides counterfeits and are now ready to pay higher prices for brands they can rely on.

Zhang Ruimin, CEO of Haier, narrated how his company learnt to adopt the Internet to reach customers a few years ago.

'We had products we thought were ready to go, flawlessly researched and developed. When they hit the market, however, results were lacklustre,' he told the website Strategy+Business. 'That got us thinking: How can we make the transition from the past, when we learned about users' needs via questionnaires and telephone calls, to the present age, when we can interact with users more directly?'[1]

'So we put forward some new concepts. For some appliances, we designed a group of various modules and invited users to select, for example, the colours and designs they wanted. In one day, we sold more than 10,000 television sets online. This made us realize that our old ways of thinking and conducting business needed an overhaul,' Zhang said.

Internet influencers have a huge market impact of around 40 per cent because they are the ones in a way that are setting trends. At the same time, through the influencer, the client company is able to gauge if the trend being created is suitable for its use or needs to be changed.

Also related comes the role of celebrities with major web presence. They send out subtle messages about what cosmetics they are wearing, what clothes or designers they like or what hairdresser they go to. This creates a sophisticated chain of influence that influences consumers at a more personal level than what a TV advertising using the same celebrity as model does.

Among content developers, video bloggers have more impact than the text bloggers although there is not enough scientific research to confirm it. Text bloggers have greater impact in messaging certain kinds of product categories such as property, automobile and financial services because they require elaborate discussion. But lifestyle products fall within the realm of video bloggers.

On a visit to India, Sinha, the Shanghai-based expert on consumer strategy, was asked by friends if there would be a market for hand-woven carpets from Mirzapur, Uttar Pradesh, in China as there is in the US. The next question he was asked was:

'*Shanghai main ek showroom kholne main kitna kharcha ayega*?'

The first line of worry is the cost of opening a showroom because Indian exporters still think in terms of brick-and-mortar shops and very few have considered digital marketing and sales. Sinha had to explain that the cost of opening a physical showroom in Shanghai would be prohibitive and he would do better to spend a much smaller amount to reach out to all Chinese cities digitally instead of being restricted to one.

Some years ago, Air New Zealand took a group of ten Chinese bloggers on its inaugural Shanghai–Auckland flight trip. Some of them were not even aviation industry bloggers. They took pictures and wrote rave reviews over the next few months, resulting in huge responses for the airlines ticketing department.

Selling on China's Internet platforms

The first thing Indian companies need to do is integrate their brand-building, their digital influence and transaction with available platforms like WeChat or Tmal.

The second is to understand the consumer needs for today and their future needs very well. The market is large and highly competitive. Not only Chinese brands but brands from several countries compete within the same segment. You have to be distinctive and unique to stand out in the crowd and this can happen if you have a good understanding about the consumer needs and trends.

With regard to market research, buying existing market research reports would be the first step. The second step is for companies to do their own research, not just at one point of time but on an ongoing basis. You can hardly boast of having consumer insight at a given time because markets and consumer tastes change every six months or sooner in China.

Buying existing market research can be useful to size up your potential and understanding of consumer trends. It should be good enough to enable you to decide which market you should launch in and whether you are ready to quickly evolve with the market. You need to have a mechanism to gain an understanding of what the consumer trends and the cultural trends are.

It is possible to leverage Indian cultural values and try to avoid the pretence of being an international brand because you are competing with both Chinese and Western brands and uniqueness is of great value. Bollywood has leveraged Bollywood and this has proved to be a huge success because Indian films provided a change from both Chinese and Hollywood movies besides presenting stories that Asian audiences can connect with. The huge popularity of Indian films offers an advantage to Indian companies both because it shows China is open to trying out new products with unique flavours and also because India's image from Bollywood movies could be a big starting point. Other aspects of Indian culture like yoga and meditation also provide unique opportunities to connect with bloggers and influencers who will then get enough content to spread the word about Indian products.

Case study: Story of an Indian in China's complex chemical business

For Telugu businessman Suresh Sirigeri, the China story began in 1995. Suresh had been importing agrochemicals from China for a few years when he decided to check out the scene in the country for himself. In any case, some Chinese companies wanted him to handle their exports and were looking for talented executives. Over the next two years, and many meetings later,

Suresh settled down in Shenzhen, capitalizing on his expertise in the agrochemicals sector.

'China was just producing organophosphorus compounds at that time, among them methyl parathion,' Suresh told me, drinking green tea in his office in Shenzhen as he discussed his early years in China. Methyl parathion is a pesticide used mainly in cotton and vegetable fields.

Both India and China were focused on developing different kinds of products at the time in the agrochemicals sector. There was 'no direct competition' as the products were different, Suresh told me.

No special licence was required at the time to import the chemicals into India—only an open general licence, or OGL. Suresh began successful sales pitches in Delhi and Mumbai, the only lucrative options at the time. By then, he had set up his company in Hong Kong, with the factory in Shenzhen. The beginning was modest.

'Initially, we were just doing it on a commission basis. So we used to tell the customer to open LCs [letters of credit]. Some Chinese suppliers, mostly factories, used to ship the products and give us the commission,' says Suresh.

Soon, Suresh was able to expand sales to other international markets. 'After India, we started selling in Thailand, and Taiwan,' he says.

I ask him why Chinese companies preferred Indian, British or American companies to sell for them instead of doing it themselves.

'If you look at the 1990s, foreign trade was through foreign trade companies. That time, even factories were not allowed directly to export without permission,' said Suresh. 'The whole restriction was entirely through banking. Bank of China was the major bank for routing all the forex deals,' he added.

China allowed exports only through state-owned companies. Then, slowly, private companies started, then factories themselves got into the import-export business.

I asked him about his prospects and key achievements since he began exporting chemicals from China in 1995.

Suresh said, 'We did new product registrations in India and started developing a part of the South American market. Recently, our interest is to get into manufacturing.' He said that earlier, traders could enter a market easily. But now, in the last ten to fifteen years, the trend is slowly changing. A lot of private companies have become manufacturers. In China, more companies started going out to explore the opportunities for their business. This entails building data along with investing time and money.

'To register for each product, we need to have studies commissioned on chemistry, toxicology data and finally bio-efficacy, so you know the field priorities in whichever countries you want to register,' Suresh says.

Having one's own knowledge dossier helps in terms of recognition and goodwill besides developing trust and ensuring regulatory compliance. The market opportunity maximizes for a company that has the capacity to both manufacture and trade. 'Because the industry trend is changing, many of the old products are being banned, new products are coming into play. Some of the new products have gone off patent, meaning they are now generic and can be easily manufactured and registered for better margins,' he says.

I cited a famous Indian hosiery manufacturer that had three factories once but has only one now. The company could not manage prices and had labour issues. Also, the next generation of owners was not willing to deal with legacy issues.

How different would Suresh's model be should the market forces become similar, I ask him.

Suresh explains, 'I see a good opportunity as Chinese companies restrict their production because of the pollution issues. In India, we can produce without compromising on pollution. We want to be very careful on that front because our country is much smaller than China and our population is almost the same.'

Pollution is not the only reason for China to restrict production. Suresh says. 'Another reason, which the Chinese media does not want to emphasize, is that nearly 82 per cent of their source of river water is the Tibetan plateau and Xinjiang as compared with India, whose sources of water are spread over the Eastern Ghats, Western Ghats etc.' The southern part of India is far from the Himalayas, but there are big rivers—the Krishna and Kaveri, for instance, without any connection with the Himalayas. India's case is very unique, in the sense that it has water sources all over the place.

'These people do not have water sources—82 per cent of the water comes from two provinces, which are politically sensitive. Polluting their scarce water systems would result in a high degree of resistance. Hence, India has a better opportunity to manufacture agrochemicals in the long run,' Suresh says. As more and more products become off-patent and available to manufacture and sell, the market opportunities will multiply.

Being in his unique position has also geared Suresh and his business for being a possible interlocutor for Chinese investments in India, particularly in the agrochemical sector. 'Because we have already built a long-term relationship with Chinese companies who are in this field a platform can be established, creating a good scope to bring in more Chinese companies to India.' The added advantage to this scenario is the goodwill and trust that Suresh's business already carries with the Chinese.

Suresh agrees about the potential for another manufacturing boom in China.

He says, 'One big challenge we faced was in 2016, when the Modi government started Make in India programme. It also impacted our industry. In our segment, agriculture ministry revised the product registration guidelines in one shot, by stopping all the files which have been already submitted under the existing guidelines.

'It was a jolt to Indian importers. Many of them changed course and started thinking of setting set up manufacturing facilities rather than just doing the production registration for import. The decision hit importers but enhanced manufacturing activity, thereby bringing down the cost of pesticides to Indian farmers,' he said.

Suresh maintains that it was not a challenge personally to him, but overall for the industry. His main challenge remained that of supply. 'You know that China's supplies are always erratic, depending on the production and the price and currency—these are the two regular challenges, you know. Every year, it passes through a kind of a cycle, not exactly a pre-determined way, but it happens.'

Overall, the agrochemicals business remains a sector with both private and state-owned players. 'Jiangsu, a major province in China, has successful private companies,' said Suresh. The government also has expressed interest in taking some stake in private companies. 'In our segment especially, China government took a very big interest by acquiring Syngenta and another company Adama, which is an Israeli company.'

Both remain top players in the market. China is a net exporter of agrochemicals, remaining three times larger than India. Indian imports of agrochemicals from China add up to USD 1.5 billion, which is half of India's domestic market valued at USD 3 billion. Imports from other countries account for 20 per cent of the market, while local manufacturers fills the rest.

Case study: Business journey from India to China to Tanzania

If you are manufacturing in China, you need to live with small margins and produce in huge quantities.

Prem Ahuja, CEO of Qingyuan Decheng Chemical Technology Co. Ltd based in south China's Guangdong province, learnt this early as he went about manufacturing watches and music speakers in south China.

Ahuja has grown far beyond his early ambitions, setting up a cement plant in China and now moving into cement manufacturing in Tanzania. Talking of his early days in the watch business, he said, 'We made a 10 per cent profit which was 10 cents. We churned out 100,000 watches a day, which left us with a good aggregate profit.' Besides, he bought movements, the interior of watches, at a slight discount to the market rate because he purchased huge quantities. That enhanced the margin by 1 per cent. Business was good.

'My staff would stay here and take orders till 3 a.m. We had a sales person, an assistant and two women, an accountant and a worker besides myself. We would eat supper in office,' he said narrating his early days in manufacturing some fifteen years ago.

Ahuja went into the chemical industry without any knowledge of chemicals. He entered without prior knowledge when he ventured into the making of watches and music speakers but picked up along the way as in the case of many entrepreneurs.

Though a lot of premium is set on acquiring advance knowledge, conducting preliminary market surveys, then pre-launch studies, there is really no clear evidence to suggest that those who depend on their hunch and dispense with advance preparations do any worse. This is the sage advice of a large number of successful entrepreneurs in different segments of the industry.

Ahuja started off making a chemical that helps the binding process of cement when mixed with sand and water. The chemical came from a petroleum company in the form of gas and had to be converted into powder form. It reduces the need for water. The ultimate cement plaster is not rough, but smooth. One can add colour to the cement and save on paint.

Ahuja laments the widespread use of old-style low-quality bricks in India when better alternatives are now available. 'I have seen the bricks used in bridge construction in Kolkata. They are so fragile, they break easily,' he says.

He has established in Yunnan province a brick factory that makes three types of bricks at the rate of 300,000 a day. The entire plant is automatic, and uses no workers. People are needed only when the bricks come out of the machines and need to be loaded on to trucks. The entire day's production is taken away in fifty trucks, leaving none behind because the market is good. There are no inventories.

The local government has provided a ring of protection, giving licences to just three brick companies in the area. Unlike in India, where there can be concentration of industries in certain places leaving everyone panting for market share, the provincial and municipal governments keep a tight leash on giving licences with respect to purely market conditions.

Authorities are also driven by considerations of pollution and limit the number of manufacturers as well as put a check on mushrooming growth of any industry in one area. Restrictions are less in low-polluting areas like garment or sofa making.

Ahuja feels secure about having properties scattered in different places of China without making arrangements for guarding them. He is convinced about the strength of the legal and policing system in this country.

Case study: When an employee takes the profit road

For those who think Chinese digital media is replete with local cultural nuances and a foreigner venturing in it would be lost in the forest of confusion, here is a story.

We are talking about two young men with no family background in business who launched themselves head-on in 2006 after some years spent working with a digital marketing company. The new company they launched after borrowing some USD 40,000 from friends and relatives has grown over fifty times in net worth today.

The men, Ravi Shankar Bose and Ranjit Singh, came to Shanghai as employees of Contests2win, an early start-up in India that decided to enter China as a joint venture with SoftBank and Siemens Mobile in the year 2000.

'I was supposed to be here for six months. But then things turned out differently. Investors felt the Indian staff needed to be in Shanghai for a much longer time,' Ravi Shankar Bose, director of Shanghai-based Fugumobile Limited, told me in an interview.

Those were the days China was starting out on the Internet business, with opportunities for growth in the internet marketing space. This was a huge learning opportunity for Bose, an electronics engineer and MBA, who handled the technical aspects of the company.

Siemens Mobile and Softbank of Japan saw an opportunity to enter the space of digital marketing at its nascent stage both in India and China. The new company with three partners was called Mobile2Win. From a demographic standpoint, aided by factors like population and maturity of the market, China was a similar market to India. It made sense to enter China as opposed to a more mature market like the UK.

The two friends, who would later become business partners, spent six years with the digital marketing team until one day when Disney decided to take over the company. Traditionally, Disney was known to enter a country through the television channel route. Chinese regulatory hurdles eliminated this strategy. Foreign companies cannot directly enter a TV channel business in China. The only way Disney could enter was through the Internet.

A lot of Chinese companies were already in the market back then and Disney wished to choose a company that had foreign management and ownership. That way Disney could make sure the accounting was transparent and there was a strong trust factor, which came from the fact that SoftBank and Siemens Mobile are well-known companies. Which is why it picked up Mobile2win in 2006.

For Bose and Singh, it was the case of an American company with a different set of needs and culture taking over the operations.

'It did not make too much sense to stick around,' says Bose. As an Internet marketing company, it was working with a lot of different brands. It had some of the local Chinese brands which were owned by P&G or Unilever. Mobile2win worked with Coca-Cola and Haier.

Once Disney acquired the company, they did not work with other brands. They wanted the entire infrastructure for their own brand.

'After the acquisition, I didn't know what to do. One choice was to go back to India. The Indian market was very good at that point of time,' he said. 'But I also felt that if I leave China at that time, I would not get another opportunity to come back here and do something.'

This is when Bose and Singh decided to try their luck with their own business plan. Their first obstacle was raising money. With a bit of help from friends and relatives, they were able to raise USD 40,000.

They started with this investment, and with a firm conviction over the contacts they had built prior to the Disney acquisition, they would be able to sign up their own former clients. Disney had refused to work with any brand other than their own, eliminating any possibility of a conflict of interest.

The workload was divided among the two friends who were now co-founders of Fugu Mobile, a name they chose as an inspiration from the fugu puffer fish, a highly poisonous delicacy in Japan which required trained chefs to serve it. It was said that even the emperor was forbidden to eat this dangerous indulgence. Besides the intrigue about the fugu fish, the co-founders also realized Japan's pioneering prowess in mobile gaming. A Japanese connotation to their own company would no doubt add a sense of semantic credibility in a way that was similar to Sony, an American-sounding Japanese company, or Haagen Dazs, a German-sounding American corporation.

For any new business starting up without major funding, allocation of money was crucial. 'It was very important that we are cash-positive in a very short amount of time,' admitted Bose. Gathering clients based on their earlier credibility was a stroke of luck; the same would not apply in execution. Business is inherently a driven group of people working together; finding the right team to hire was the second challenge.

When Fugu began operations in 2006, Chinese education did not have the same reputation in the world that it carries today. Some remote villages did not have access to the Internet and people migrated from small towns to work in the big cities. This was a striking similarity with India. Moreover, people coming from different places carried a drive and ambition to do well.

Fugu would be perceived as a company by foreigners, Indians to be specific, and Indians can teach you software.

To address the staffing challenge, Bose and Singh went straight to the source. NIIT had been present in China for some time and a request for their students would prove to be ideal. It obliged and a small office was set up, with a strength of five people. Working with a strong team would ensure good results with a new client, and more business. A unique formation was achieved. Both the founders were aware of the Chinese method of precise execution and the Indian strength in research and development. Striking a balance between the two would make the company a formidable entity in the still newly developing market.

With a bit of effort aided by a stroke of luck, Fugu managed to bag Mercedes AMG as their first client. This gave a big boost to both the business and the overall morale of the workforce, many of whom were car enthusiasts. Maserati followed, which gave an aspirational edge to the company employees.

The most striking quality of their own workforce, of which both Bose and Singh remain proud, was discovered when a client decided to venture into a solution that could work for the iPhone, which had just been launched by Apple in 2007. Admitting to the client that they had no iPhone expert on board would not be a wise choice. Hiring an expert was the natural option. Most of the staff that had joined earlier from NIIT had only worked on Nokia and Sony Ericsson phones, a rapidly fading technology. What surprised both the co-founders was the willingness of the existing employees to work on the new iPhone technology.

'You have one week,' Bose proclaimed to them in 2007, after which they would have hired an iPhone expert. The team agreed and delivered. This motivation and excitement to work with new technologies have remained a driving force and part of the company ethos to date. The teams followed the same style of execution with WeChat during the dawn of Chinese social media.

The Chinese drive to learn and execute, coupled with the Indian strategic mind has led the company to be a respected market force today. Rapidly enough that they did not seek investment from any large company. They remain an independent entity today with a possible market valuation of roughly 25–30 million dollars.

Most of the staff that joined Fugu in 2006 has remained with them today. They have developed a flexible work ethic, which allows family time. Modern corporations are moving away from the age-old Western capitalist concept of time cards and employees sacrificing their lives for the company. Both Bose and Singh are aware of this new change and have established a working relationship with their employees that capitalizes on their personalities as much as their efficiency.

'We don't want brilliant people, we want good people,' says Bose.

It would be interesting to find out where he thought Fugumobile will be heading in the next two years.

'We have been looking at opportunities where we could expand to other countries. We see how fast China is still evolving. China is not really done with the market being completely matured. It is expanding very fast,' he said. 'We feel that we are going to be

China focused. But we are going to be opening at different places. If you look at east China, it is completely different, almost like a different country from the central or western part of China. There is an opportunity in the tier 3 and tier 5 cities of China, he added.

5

DEAL-MAKING WHILE NAVIGATING CHINESE CULTURE

Knowledge of local culture is an essential tool for negotiation in any country. This is more important in countries like China, Japan and South Korea—a major draw of foreign businessmen—because the thinking process of people in these places is closely linked to their cultural mores even though they may have travelled the world and even been exposed to Indian people.

In this section, we will discuss nine different cultural mores of the Chinese that every Indian businessman or businesswoman must keep in mind at every stage of business, from seeking quotations, checking quality, negotiating and booking deals to following up. It is easy to kill a deal by making a few involuntary mistakes even at the point when it is about to be completed.

Indian business executives dealing with Chinese companies in China or in India or any other part of the world may find it useful to understand their negotiation techniques and cultural ways.

We will also talk to two Indians who have been engaged in business negotiations in China for many years. Let's start by understanding a few cultural rules to keep in mind while dealing with the Chinese.

You would be surprised to often find Chinese speaking flawless English, though they do so slowly to give themselves time to first form thoughts and sentences in their mind in Mandarin and then translating them.

What comes through is a very cautious and understated response. For instance, 'maybe you are right. I don't know' might actually mean that the speaker does not agree with you at all. And if they don't like a dish or something you show or offer, a Chinese person might simply say, 'It's so-so.'

There's no guile in this. It comes from a long culture of never rejecting something to the face. There is always an attempt to stay polite while being clear. Being understated appears to be safer than being explicit and loud.

The problem arises when a foreigner thinks that 'so-so' means 'yes' or 'doable' and ends up making wrong decisions. We will dwell more on these aspects later in this section. Let us now move to the nine Chinese cultural mores that must be kept in mind when negotiating with them.

Guanxi (personal connections)

In essence, guanxi means a person's social capital, which in China is most worthy of acquiring. A person, whatever his position in life, must acquire this capital to be respected and trusted.

In some sense, this is a combination of the Western idea of networking and the Indian *jaan-pehchan* (meaning acquaintance) or, as a Gujarati would say, *audhkhan*, or nepotism, conveying the idea of *laag-baag* (using influence). Indian businessmen who deal with credit as a routine aspect of the business would understand the role that trust plays in capital formation. Connections with friends, family members, people who come from his country or province and speak Chinese with the same distinct dialect and the network of business associates all add up to make a businessman's social capital in China.

In the race to acquire some business or when it is necessary to get out of a difficult situation, guanxi comes to the rescue. Friends and associations pool in not just their capital resources but the combined strength of each other's social capital to help out a member of this loose club.

Foreigners often wonder how they can enter this tight circle to do business with the Chinese and get their work done. We will discuss this soon. Meanwhile, it must be noted that the globalization of Chinese business has somewhat diluted the influence of guanxi. But it continues to survive and thrive in ways that were not imagined before easy international travel was born.

Zhongjian ren (the intermediary)

You need someone to introduce you when you come to China without a past record of business or contacts. He's your point person in a world where you have no guanxi.

China has some bitter memories of being exploited by foreigners—the Opium War has not been forgotten—resulting in some suspicion and mistrust concerning *wai guo ren* or outside-country people, as the Chinese describe foreigners.

As with any foreigner, an Indian must be ready—and not get unduly miffed—to be eyed and heard with some distrust. It's a bit too much to demand trust in the first couple of meetings, anyway.

In the Chinese way, trust moves through the conveyer belt of the zhongjian ren, who will use his own time-tested guanxi to make the other party trust you. A good intermediary comes at a price, not just because he has knowledge of the local market and its players, but also because he is investing his social capital in a deal. If it works, his influence goes up. If it sours, he has a lot to lose.

The Chinese are uncomfortable with people getting to the point and on with the task of business from the moment they meet. Americans and Europeans have had to unlearn generations of culture of diving straight to the core aspect of business without wasting anyone's time.

For the Chinese, it is more important to identify the decision maker in a business group or company and size up his personality.

People run companies, not the other way round, even in the age of robotics. Hence, the need for what some scholars have described as 'non-task sounding', which is trying to get to know each other though conversation, drinking and eating together.

Visiting Indian business executives often boast about the 'red carpet treatment' they are given and taken to meals with a variety of forty to sixty dishes served. Half a dozen smartly dressed and nice-looking waitresses try to make diners feel welcome. Some visitors indulge themselves, and some fret over the excess, wondering if the additional cost will show in the quotations.

The wiser and experienced folks know they are being watched with shrewd eyes, which are accustomed to watching foreigners from different countries. You are being read to gauge your mood, intonations, facial expression and body language, all of which goes into making an impression. The guiding hand of zhongjian ren can be very useful.

Shehui dengji (social status)

Chinese are extremely sensitive about the status of a person negotiating a deal. Sending a junior to discuss business with an important businessman is asking for the doors to be closed. Similarly, rushing the top executive of your company to discuss matters with junior officials on the Chinese side would show you as an overeager company desperately looking for a deal. Chinese never show desperation and are wary of those that do.

Initial negotiations usually reach a point when executives enjoying the same status might meet and understand each other. The Indian company must be represented by someone at the same standing as the Chinese representative.

Chinese top-level executives would not discuss the nitty-gritty details of business deals, which is left to the lower staff. They will not get into price bargaining either. Top-level executives are the big-picture men, they take a holistic view in the light of their companies' overall international strategy and the deal being negotiated is one part of it. More important, they want you to regard them as someone special and different from their associates.

Renji hexie (interpersonal harmony)

Chinese believe that being polite is not just about good nature but it is also a business tool. Harmony and not a clash of words even when there are differences is the way to go.

One Chinese saying that explains this is: 'Sweet temper and friendliness produce money.' Harmony comes when both sides show respect for each other, and treat each other as equals.

Many visiting Indians are surprised to find total strangers whom they have met for business for the first time toasting them as if they have known each other from an earlier life. 'Long live our cooperation. Let us toast to each other,' your Chinese host may say. He may seem to be exaggerating a relationship that has just begun, if at all.

In his mind, he is making his contribution towards renji hexie, or interpersonal harmony, with you. This sense of harmony and meeting of minds is more important to many Chinese than written deals.

A section of Indian businessmen also believes in this principle. A quote often attributed to Mahatma Gandhi, who hailed from a business family in Porbandar, is: 'A customer is the most important visitor on our premises. He is not dependent on us. We are dependent on him. He is not an interruption in our work. He is the purpose of it. He is not an outsider in our business. He is part of it. We are not doing him a favour by serving him. He is doing us a favour by giving us an opportunity to do so.'

Zhengti guannian (holistic thinking)

Indian businessmen, like the Westerners, may look at different aspects of the business such as availability of goods, quality, price and delivery schedules, and prefer to discuss them separately.

On the other hand, the Chinese business executive would prefer to look at the situation in its totality with all aspects considered at one time before deciding if he wants to take the next step. He might ask unexpected questions concerning your requirements, the decision makers in your company, the associates that you deal with and then go into every bit of the business on hand. In effect, he is sizing you up as well as estimating the value of your business offer to him.

Such lengthy discussions, which may seem irrelevant at certain times, could be a test of patience for an Indian business executive. It's better to be prepared with the right responses.

Jiejian (thrift)

The Chinese may seem calculating but this must be seen in the light of their culture for thrift and refusal to spend money wastefully.

China, like India, has a high rate of savings. The faith in the importance of saving may seem to be in conflict with the big wining and dining events hosted by Chinese companies—which has not been curtailed to a good extent—unless we understand that those expenses are regarded as business necessity.

Mianzi ('face' or social image)

Mianzi is about dignity and the need to make sure you don't hurt anyone's sense of self-worth.

Let me tell you a personal story here. I had a Chinese businessman friend with considerable influence, and I learnt quite a bit from him. One day he sent me a gift which I thought was expensive. Being a journalist, I felt I shouldn't accept it and returned it. I lost the friend. He did not want to see me again.

I later consulted a Chinese professor to find out if I made a mistake in my relationship.

'Big mistake. You have caused him to lose face. Even worse, if his staff came to know of it,' the professor explained. When I asked for detailed explanation, he said. 'You friend was showing you respect by sending that gift. Respect and love are shown with well-priced gifts, not cheap ones. By rejecting, you committed a big mistake. You showed him disrespect and conveyed that he is not worthy of your respect.'

This story should give an idea about how important the issue of face is. A man or woman's reputation and social standing rests on saving face. If someone causes embarrassment, even unintentionally, it can mean a setback or cancellation of business negotiations.

In China, people go out of the way to save another person's face, even praise and pamper him to fill him with a high sense of self-worth instead of causing harm to his dignity. Emotional outbursts, display of anger, frustration, or aggression at the negotiation table, can result in loss of face, and the end of a deal.

The Chinese feel that a key aspect of mutual understanding is endurance and avoiding bitterness of any kind to cloud business judgement.

Delay as negotiating tactic

Foreign businessmen visiting businesses across different provinces are confounded by certain breaks in discussions and the Chinese penchant for asking the same question as if he did not understand when you explained something the first time around.

Is he really stupid or is he fishing for additional information or simply watching if you are consistent in your description of your products, services or requirements? Maybe playing dumb is a smarter way of making money instead of exhibiting one's knowledge and capabilities.

Chinese may use lulls during negotiation to consider any new information or develop more questions. They have learnt that investment in time pays off.

People who represent

What matters is whether the right people, with knowledge of products and company and ability to influence decision-making, are appreciated. A China-born or Chinese-speaking executive is preferred over those who use interpreters.

What Indians doing business in China have learnt

'In my view, Chinese negotiation framework means understanding and accommodating the Chinese-style approach to craft a strategic plan that works on the local level. And preparation of negotiation is quite important in order to gain insight into the negotiating partner's situation, intent and capabilities, and to identify areas of focus for discussions,' Vijay Singh, country head for China for the Ispat Group, told me in an interview in Beijing.

Singh believes there are three factors worth considering:

- Knowing your customer thoroughly and doing all ground work by collecting information on the company through your contacts and wisdom.
- A SWOT analysis to identify an Indian company's strength, weakness, opportunities and threats in the Chinese business scene. It may be significantly different from the analysis done back home.
- Aligning internal organizational resources to work most effectively in Chinese-style negotiations. It is always wise to speak less and listen more carefully because simple-sounding discussions may actually be the start of complex negotiations. It never helps to show your hand in a premature manner.

M.H. Pastakia, an advisor guiding Indian businessmen seeking deals in China, has some interesting thoughts to share about how an Indian buyer of Chinese machinery and other products should handle the process of introduction, initial discussion, negotiation on price and quality and follow-up with a Chinese seller.

'Depending on the product or technology, it is very necessary to make the Chinese understand what is to be bought. Also a good introduction with possibilities of long-term supply business helps to get the Chinese more interested in offering their best quality and support,' Pastakia said, sitting in Beijing's Taj Pavilion restaurant, which he owns.

He said negotiations on price, quality and other issues are needed but haggling is not the most important part. 'Research is necessary to understand the market price of the product by trying two to three suppliers. Over-negotiating tends to kill the business,' he said.

Referring to the mindset issues of Indian buyers, Pastakia said, 'There is a misconception that good negotiation can bring down the price to very low levels. Most Chinese businessmen will negotiate as much as the buyer wants (so as not to lose his business to others) and provide the final product, which may be low in quality from what was first required but worth the amount finally negotiated at.'

Also, he says, it is imperative to insist on the quality standards when negotiating. Follow-up is normally only if there are any repeat orders. A Chinese consultant may be necessary if the product or the business deal needs an expert from that field.

The prevalent wrong assumptions with which many Indian businessmen enter China is that they are dealing with cheap products at half the price.

Most products of quality standards are cheaper in China than in other parts of the world by about 15–30 per cent but not at half the price.

Chinese don't usually convey their decision to do a deal until the dinner is laid out and enjoyed heartily accompanied with laughter and bonhomie and lots of *ganbei*, or bottoms-up with glasses of wine.

How should a vegetarian and non-drinker handle a dinner invitation by a potential supplier/customer?

Dinner invitations end up with a lot of 'exotic' non-vegetarian dishes and alcohol. The Chinese like to have a good dinner with a fair amount of alcohol. Some may feel bored they are if not accompanied in drinking and eating. 'If possible, go with a colleague who can do the drinking or "Cheers" on your behalf with the suppliers,' advises Pastakia.

Whatever the political differences between India and China, Indians living in this country are at ease and do not face any more hurdles than they would have faced in India.

"We feel at ease in this country because Chinese values are very similar to Indian ones, especially in the importance given to family relationships and to education," Ramakrishna Velamuri, Professor of Entrepreneurship at the China Europe International Business School in Shanghai, told me.

The huge success of Bollywood movies in China shows that the local audience can easily connect with Indian stories.

"We have always found the Chinese people to be very welcoming and warm. This is even more the case in smaller cities," he said.

How to use interpreters without incurring losses in translation

There are two aspects worth keeping in mind. Quite often, a visiting Indian would think and express himself in complex ways. If a buyer likes a machine and is also comfortable with the price, he will go on to explain why he likes it and why he thinks the price could have been lower. This may be a show of transparency from the viewpoint of the Indian buyer but too much discussion would sometimes leave the Chinese counterpart confused.

There is a communication issue and things must be said in bite sizes. An instant flow of words and ideas can leave the interpreter struggling to grasp and panting for breath. The interpreter must be at ease for him or her to communicate to the Chinese businessman.

The simple solution is to speak in short sentences, one thought at a time, in the manner young reporters are trained to write reports without assaulting the reader with a load of information in each sentence. Each sentence must express one thought.

6

BUILDING INFRASTRUCTURE AND INFLUENCE

In its second avatar, the Modi government will have to decide whether it wants to bite the silver bullet, which may be filled with nectar or have traces of poison. It has to decide whether it wants to accept China's Belt and Road Initiative, or BRI, with its offer of developing much-needed infrastructure but can also exacerbate India's security concerns.

No one doubts that the BRI can change India's economic landscape with connectivity infrastructure like railways, roads and ports, which the Chinese are more than eager to finance, provided of course, the contracts for construction and machinery purchases go to them. India has to think how much foreign debt it wants to bear and also examine the security angle.

A question that I ask Chinese friends trying to convince me about its high-growth potential is whether China would accept a version of the BRI that covers India's hinterland states and leaves out the entire border region between the two countries. Put differently, would Beijing agree to a BRI that has no cross-border linkages with India?

Chinese scholars do not want to discuss this question for two reasons. One of BRI's goals is to transport Chinese goods to India through the land border via Nepal, Ladakh or Arunachal Pradesh and leaving out the border region would not serve its trade goals. According to some experts, cross-border connectivity starting from and built by China will definitely give it some sort of military advantage and make India vulnerable to some extent in the future.

The grandiose BRI project covers more than sixty countries, including those in Europe, besides Asia, Africa and Latin America. Beijing hopes to redraw the world economic map, with BRI countries forming an economic block that would challenge the domination of the US and help China leapfrog to number one position. This projection is backed by analysis by some Western think tanks that see the US receding to the second position in economic strength somewhere between 2030 and 2050. The core of BRI is Chinese-financed and -constructed connectivity infrastructure and electricity projects across the globe.

China is competing for influence in the world with the US. Its extensive trade has made it the most important trade partner for more than half of the world. As the world's biggest trader, China is stronger in terms of trade influence than the US.

Another factor emerging as a major influence generator is Beijing's ability to send its construction and engineering companies to build infrastructure projects across dozens of different countries. Chinese leaders are looking at both strategic and business advantages that can be built by combining the influence of its trade and infrastructure-building capabilities with diplomacy and overawing military presence. Each feeds into the other, making China stronger in both economic and military strength.

It is in the context of this overall picture that the BRI proposal announced by Chinese President Xi Jinping in 2013 needs to be seen. It has been packaged and sold to leaders of dozens of foreign governments as China's development outreach to help poorer countries replicate its model of impressive infrastructure growth and connectivity.

Many leaders in Eastern Europe, Asia, Africa and Latin America find themselves drawn, even lusting, to grab China's offering, which appears like a box of sweets. Beijing is offering to build massive

Powering the Belt and Road Initiative

China builds and invests in power plants and grid infrastructure worldwide

planned/under construction — completed — no. of projects: >1

Project value: > 100 million USD

FOSSIL-FUEL POWER PLANTS* — *at least: 350 MW

RENEWABLE ENERGY POWER PLANTS** — **at least: 200 MW

NUCLEAR POWER PLANTS

GRID EXTENSION/ DISTRIBUTION NETWORK EXPANSION

TRANSMISSION LINE (PLANNED/UNDER CONSTRUCTION)

TRANSMISSION LINE (COMPLETED)

INVESTMENT IN GRID OPERATORS (COMPLETED)

PAKISTAN

FLAGSHIP PROJECTS IN PAKISTAN

2 billion USD
Port Qasim Coal Power Plant
Fossil fuel (completed)

1.4 billion USD
Karot Hydro Power Plant
Renewable energy (under construction)

CHINA'S ENERGY FLAGSHIP PROJECTS

2 billion USD
Pacific Hydro (Australia)
Renewable energy (completed)

1.8 billion USD
Patuakhali Power Plant (Bangladesh)
Fossil fuel (planned)

1 billion USD
Addis Ababa-Grand Renaissance Dam (Ethiopia)
Transmission line (completed)

760 million USD
EETC Transmission Network (Egypt)
Grid expansion (under construction)

360 million USD
ADMIE (Greece)
Grid investment (completed)

infrastructure projects—the likes of which these countries can only dream of—and even finance them. Critics, and this includes India and the US, have warned these countries of piling up massive debt that they will not be able to pay. But the current leaders of developing countries are more bothered about showing their capability to produce results than bothering about future debt. Legacy issues don't bother leaders across Asia, Africa and Latin America who are engaged in political fire-fighting, winning elections and enforcing dictatorships.

The reality is much simpler compared to the complexities of Chinese propaganda for the Silk Road Plan, now called BRI, as well as the counterpoints raised by Washington and objections from New Delhi. The history of the Silk Road bears this out.

'It is no accident that the Silk Road is named only for the main product travelling westwards from China. There is no compatible mention of whatever was moving east along the same route (in reality nothing much of any great interest). In more recent times merchantmen sailed home to Europe, laden with another highly desirable commodity—exquisite vases and dishes, bowls and teacups of Chinese porcelain. Again, it is no accident that in several European languages such items, wherever they may now come from, are known as China,' Bamber Gascoigne wrote while discussing the early years of the Silk Road from the first century BC to the first few hundred years after the birth of Christ.[1]

In his book *China's Asian Dream*, Tom Miller draws parallels with the East India Company, which went to India and elsewhere to conduct trade but ended up establishing the British Empire.

'No one is predicting a Chinese Raj but Beijing's resolve to defend both its core national interests and rights of its citizens means that non-interference in foreign affairs is no longer an option. As economic realities push China towards a great-power status, China will have to project more political and military muscle across Asia—whether it wants to or not,' Miller wrote after travelling through a dozen countries on the BRI route map.

The most prominent aspect of the BRI is the USD 60 billion China–Pakistan Economic Corridor (CPEC) which 'will pass through a portion of Pakistan-occupied Kashmir', which India considers as its own.

India sees CPEC as a challenge to its sovereignty. 'The so-called China-Pakistan Economic Corridor violates India's sovereignty and territorial integrity. No country can accept a project that ignores its core concerns on sovereignty and territorial integrity,' said Ministry of External Affairs spokesperson Raveesh Kumar.[2]

Since then, India has stuck to its stance that it cannot participate in BRI because it is a programme that will hurt India's sovereignty. China has done all it can to persuade India by offering goodies as well as posing challenges by getting more Indian neighbours like Sri Lanka and Nepal to sign up on BRI projects. India is being threatened with isolation by its own neighbours—including Bangladesh, Myanmar and Afghanistan, which has been offered generous assistance by China—who happen to be close political and trade partners.

'My view has always been that BRI, given its decisive top-down backing, was always going to happen—regardless of what other countries might or might not want. China is flush with cash in the same way as the US was in the early-twentieth century and Japan was in the early 1980s. A deluge of overseas investment was always on the cards,' Sourabh Gupta, senior fellow at the Institute of China America Studies in Washington, told me in an interview.

India's best choice is to try and shape the contours of this investment to India's advantage in South Asia. Gupta favours India cooperating with BRI with regard to the BCIM (Bangladesh, China, India and Myanmar) corridor and not the CPEC on the western side. It makes sense not to cooperate and uncut India's position in an area where it has sovereignty-related reservations.

'But elsewhere, it is not a good idea to remain weeded to our grievance. We must pursue our interests. And if that means cooperating with BRI, so be it—especially when every other developing country in South Asia and South East Asia has signed on to the Initiative,' said Gupta adding, 'Keeping an arms-length distance is not wise neighbourhood policy.'

There has been a murmur of support in some sections of the Indian elite who are frustrated by our lacklustre record in attracting FDI from China in absolute terms, although 2018 numbers on FDI may look impressive compared to even worse performance in the past. The Chinese have also relentlessly kept up their propaganda efforts, trying to change opinion in favour of BRI while targeting a large section of Indian influencers in politics, industry, official circles and the media.

The reason why India has not done well in attracting sufficient FDI is different.

'The key reason India has failed to attract sufficient FDI is the failure of the successive governments to introduce and implement major land, labour, education and taxation reforms,' said Mohan Malik, professor on Asian security at the Asia-Pacific Center for Security Studies in Honolulu.

'I would question the underlying assumption that China would let India grow into an economic powerhouse or as a peer competitor of China. China's trade and investment policy towards smaller countries are different from its policy towards major powers or great power rivals such as the United States, Japan and India,' Malik said.

Countries that are seen as rivals or geopolitical competitors of China often tend to accumulate huge trade deficits with China, and this is not a coincidence, he said. Beijing is keen to ensure dependence of its rivals on its economic power and would not be interested in fostering their growth. It is a different issue when China is backing non-rivals like Sri Lanka, Pakistan or even Greece.

He thinks that Beijing's beggar-thy-rival policy is also evident in its denial of market access to the US, India and other countries that can take advantage of better access.

It is wrong to cite FDI as a reason for supporting BRI.

India is set to overtake China as the most populous country and the world's largest market, in number of consumers, for the first time in the millennium.

India is not opposed to taking Chinese help for developing its infrastructure. In fact, the Ministry of Railways has given seven orders for railway equipment to Chinese companies who are now being involved in bigger projects like medium- and high-speed rail networks. The question is whether India should open up the sensitive border issue and allow Chinese roads to come in across the Himalayas, even though the border dispute remains unsolved.

Is India overdoing its resistance to the Belt and Road Initiative?

The main issue for India concerns its sovereignty. BRI's most successful implementation is taking place in the USD 60 billion CPEC, which has resulted in the building of some major roads and power stations in Pakistan with Chinese money. A part of CPEC falls in Pakistan Occupied Kashmir, which India claims as its own.

China has tried to overcome India's protestations about CPEC violating its sovereignty by pointing out that that the project was being implemented for the sake of poor people in Pakistan. Surprisingly, China itself plays the sovereignty card when it comes to several land and sea disputes. It claims ownership of the Taiwan island, although it has its own flag, currency and military. Beijing blames the US for hurting its sovereignty every time Washington sells military equipment to Taiwan. China is also engaged in sovereignty disputes with Japan, Vietnam, Indonesia and Philippines over ownership of islands in East China Sea and the South China Sea.

There is an emerging viewpoint in a section of the Indian elite, in business, politics and media, that India should permit the BRI. This view is driven by a few factors:

- Frustration that India has failed to attract sufficient FDI.
- The desire to grab Chinese capital and infrastructure advantages, which is not possible due to New Delhi's opposition to BRI.

- The fear that neighbouring countries like Pakistan, Nepal, Bangladesh and Sri Lanka will surge ahead in terms of infrastructure and become bases for Chinese manufacturing, which would give tremendous competition to Indian business.
- The belief that China's military would be less aggressive if India becomes a major market for it, particularly when Beijing is engaged in a trade war.

Let's start with the last, and most unorthodox, among the factors mentioned earlier. Will accepting the BRI make China's People's Liberation Army less aggressive towards India?

'Yes, and it could work in two instances. If India becomes an important base for Chinese producers to export to third-country markets or even back to China, Beijing will be more circumspect about boundary matters militarily,' Sourabh Gupta, Senior Fellow at the Institute of China US Studies in Washington, told me in an interview. 'More importantly, if India becomes a large final consumer of Chinese products—not only for handsets but for a range of other white goods too, the fear of consumer boycotts could also feed back into prudence on the boundary. That said, though, this argument should not be taken too far. Geo-economics will only go so far in staying China's geopolitical hand when a real-time contingency arises. That's simply how China's statecraft works,' he added.

In other words, allowing China and its construction programme and Chinese companies greater access in India may soften China's security aggressiveness, whatever there is. But it would not completely stop the People's Liberation Army for fighting for what it sees as China's 'core interests' in times of exigencies.

It must be stated in plain terms that China will not give up its claim over Arunachal Pradesh in north-east India and border troubles can re-emerge from time to time whether or not India adopts the BRI. At the same time, it is absurd to be over-suspicious about BRI when all the neighbouring countries are developing their infrastructure and economic capabilities.

Many Indians scoff at the possibility of Pakistan, Nepal, Bangladesh, Myanmar and Sri Lanka emerging as economic forces with Chinese support and then snatching off business opportunities from Indian companies. But this is an emerging reality and Indian business should be ready to further lose their influence in the neighbouring countries because local businesses in these countries may have gone through some blood infusion by the Chinese.

'CPEC could help revive Pakistan's economy. But if it moves ahead without more thorough debate in parliament and provincial legislatures and consultation with locals, it will deepen friction between the federal centre and periphery, roil provinces already long neglected, widen social divides and potentially create new sources of conflict,' the International Crisis Group said in a June 2018 analysis.

Mohan Malik, Professor of Strategic Studies at the UAE's National Defense College, warns that India should be careful about accepting BRI. 'The history of China–India interactions cautions against raising unrealistic expectations,' he told me in an email interview. 'I would question the underlying assumption that China would let India grow into an economic powerhouse or as a peer competitor of China,' he said, while pointing out that India is the only major power whose relative power vis-à-vis China is set to grow over the next few decades.

Malik, who was earlier at the Asia-Pacific Center for Security Studies in Honolulu, made the interesting observation that China's disputes with Japan and the United States have not lessened, although it has half a trillion-dollar worth of trade with these countries.

'Therefore, a USD 100 to USD 200 billion trade with India in the coming years is not going to make them sing *Kumbaya* (the campfire classic) or make China behave less aggressive militarily towards India,' he said.

Arunachal Pradesh, which is three times the size of Taiwan, is at the core of the boundary dispute between India and China. China claims ownership over the state, calling it 'South Tibet' and making it a sovereignty issue.

'An increasingly powerful China has no incentive to soften its stand on territorial sovereignty issues. History shows that trading partners can still go to war,' Malik said.

Much of Chinese investments either goes to the developed West or to its old or potential geostrategic allies like Cambodia, Myanmar and Pakistan and some others located along China's vital sea lines of communication.

Gupta said, 'So bottom line: New Delhi should buy into the economic opportunity to reorient BRI's strategic dynamic to its advantage instead of looking at it as a strategic challenge.'

It will be a tough trapeze dance for New Delhi. 'Of course, I agree with those who feel this is too fine a balance to walk. Yes, it is a delicate and difficult balance to tread. But I think Indian diplomacy is capable of treading this fine line,' said Gupta.

Is non-decision a safe bet?

Whatever India's misgivings, it cannot watch Beijing economically arm its neighbours like Pakistan, Nepal, Myanmar, Bangladesh and Sri Lanka, and make itself vulnerable to business pressures in the near future.

There is also a growing restlessness in the Indian business community which is worried about missing out on new investment opportunities and might also make this an excuse for its inability to grow as fast as other countries. The government has reasons to worry about domestic pressure on the issue, which is pouring out in the media and might soon be reflected in Parliament.

'There is a danger too of just sitting outside the framework contemptuously when practically every other country in South, Southeast and Central Asia has signed on. And even more dangerous if BRI actually succeeds in some/many of its projects,' Gupta said.

He pointed out that there is a lot of talk about the Chinese project failure at Hambantota in Sri Lanka. But nobody speaks of the Colombo Container Terminal Success and the possibility of the Chinese-backed Colombo Port City project proving to be a success in the coming years.

'And these success stories won't remain invisible in perpetuity. Better to hedge our bets by participating with—not within—BRI in third-country markets, just as Japan and France have signed on,' he said.

China has been telling the world that it is keen to uplift infrastructure in poor and developing countries because it would resolve the world's problems and be a 'win-win solution' for all countries along the BRI map. Note that most projects under BRI are connectivity infrastructure that will allow Chinese goods to travel across the world and create markets for its companies. China is supporting Pakistan in order to get access to its Gwadar Port and thus link its Xinjiang region to the Arabian Sea. The reason why Beijing is also investing in power projects is because it was a major political demand in Pakistan and also nothing moves without electricity.

'Excess capacity is a major motivator behind China's Belt and Road. As the president of China's Development Bank said in May, "What can we do with the excess production capacity? We can only send it abroad,"' Jonathan Hillman, senior researcher at the Centre for Strategic and International Studies, told me.

'China's ability to build things far exceeds its domestic needs, so it wants to find foreign markets. It really needs to downsize some of these bloated firms, but that is politically difficult.'

Talking about the claimed advantages of Pakistan's Gwadar Port, Hillman said that a lot of it was hype. 'The plans for building a pipeline and railway from Gwadar into China are pipe dreams. Even if those projects were completed, they would only replace a small fraction of the trade in goods and energy that is carried by the sea,' he said.

Beijing has argued it needs alternative land routes for its goods because of the problems in certain sea routes and future military escalation leading to closure of the traditional routes. But analysts said such a situation where sea routes are closed and land routes are safe is difficult to imagine. In any case, the Gwadar Port is located in the highly charged and terror-prone Balochistan region of Pakistan.

'CPEC's connectivity is quite weak. Even though it is called a "corridor", the vast majority of CPEC project activity is within Pakistan, rather than connecting China and Pakistan. The Karakoram Highway has been around for a long time, and even after it's upgraded will still be closed for several months every year due to snow,' Hillman said.

BJP national general secretary Ram Madhav said during a visit to China that the Indian government planned to link the north-east region with Chittagong in Bangladesh.[3] As he was speaking in Beijing, it was widely seen as a sign that New Delhi was changing its stance towards BRI and was ready to accommodate it in some ways if it helped India's strategy on developing connectivity along the Bangladesh, China, India, Myanmar corridor or BCIM.

'We have not attempted connecting north-east with China. Our vision was that they are natural neighbours. North-east has [a long] boundary with China,' PTI quoted Madav as saying at a press conference in Beijing. 'South West China can use north-east as a hub to go to Indian Ocean through Chittagong. We have not explored much. We only thought through Sikkim we can give access to China to the Indian Ocean through Kolkata port. But this (Chittagong port) is also an excellent opportunity,' the BJP leader said.

Chinese scholars, including those employed in government think tanks, expressed delight over the statement and welcomed it. Such is the Chinese eagerness for Indian support to BRI.

Madhav was accompanied by senior Cabinet ministers from Assam, Tripura and Nagaland during his visit to the southern Chinese city of Guangzhou when they met Indian and Chinese businessmen in early 2019.

'If the Indian government confirms an invitation to China to participate in its northeastern projects, that means India is shifting toward China's Belt and Road Initiative,' Zhao Gancheng, director of the Shanghai Institute for the International Studies Centre for Asia-Pacific Studies in Beijing, told the state-run *Global Times*.[4]

The same report quoted Lan Jianxue, an associate research fellow at the China Institute of International Studies, as saying that China might get involved in the kind of project Madhav suggested if it did not involve any territorial dispute.

'Cooperation between India and China is promising, but India needs to banish any vestiges of a cold war mentality,' Lan said.

Chinese attraction for India's construction and infrastructure industry, including the influence-building real-estate business, has forced the world to sit up and take notice.

Some countries have realized China desperately needs to prove itself as the leader of the world. Its ambition of replacing the United States in the economic arena means that it will go to great lengths to find places where it can send its construction and engineering companies to build much-needed infrastructure and establish its influence in the process.

Amid calls from the US about being careful of the risks involved in BRI and a lot of reluctance among most European nations to join it came the somewhat startling news that Italy has decided to participate in China's global dream. Italy recently became the first member of the Group of Seven, or the wealthy club of G7 countries, to join China's BRI programme, much to the chagrin of its European neighbours in the early months of 2019.

For Rome, it was a simple matter of obtaining Chinese funds and expertise to rebuild its infrastructure and an economy which is struggling under a debt crisis. This was a political victory for China, faced with widespread cynicism towards BRI, and Beijing tweaked the contract package heavily to win the deal, according to diplomatic circles. This was China's second biggest foray in Europe after one of its companies acquired the Port of Piraeus in Greece to facilitate easy movement of its goods-laden containers.

Bangladesh Prime Minister Sheikh Hasina visited Beijing in July 2019 for a few days and returned to Dhaka with a handful of documents containing Chinese offers to extend assistance worth a colossal USD 31 billion for building infrastructure projects. This is the second biggest assistance offer under BRI after Chinese President Xi Jinping granted a USD 60 billion package for the CPEC.

Beijing has also caused excitement in Kathmandu with offers to build linkage roads and railway lines while supporting Nepal's hydrological dam projects. In both cases, it has taken away the initiative from India which has been sitting over several assistance proposals from these neighbours for decades.

At the core of the problem is not political will as media columnists routinely talk about. It runs deeper and involves a government's ability to make business sense of diplomacy for domestic companies. With a one-party rule driven by capitalistic passion, China's diplomatic missions have been able to work hand in hand with their companies, often negotiating on their behalf across different countries. This strength is behind Beijing's drive to implement the BRI programme, stupendous as it is, across the world.

The Indian scene is different. Indian construction and engineering firms like L&T and subsidiaries of Indian Railways and Indian Oil Corporation (IOC) have gained a few orders overseas but not big enough to make foreign engagement lucrative for Indian companies.

The Indian diplomatic service is not trained to carry out economic functions, leave aside handholding for companies seeking opportunities abroad. The government besmirched its image when it failed to defend an IOC oil exploration project in Vietnam against extremely loud protests from China which said India was interfering with its sovereignty by drilling in an area off the shore of Vietnam, which Beijing claims as its own. Incidentally, the area concerned is also claimed by Vietnam, and IOC was in partnership with a government company in Hanoi.

The new move involves flooding Bangladesh with Chinese funds, something Dhaka has not been accustomed to after years of haggling with India for small parcels of financial aid. The move will have implications for New Delhi's plans to link north-east India with the Chittagong port in Bangladesh. The coming months will show how the plan works out.

Bangladesh Prime Minister Sheikh Hasina was accorded a red-carpet welcome, followed by a salute of honour by armed forces at the picturesque Great Hall of the People, which houses the Chinese Parliament. She sent out a signal about the importance of China when she made it the destination of her first foreign visit after her recent re-election.

She presided over the signing of nine agreements between the two countries, covering areas like economic and technical cooperation and investments in electricity development, tourism and culture. Documents signed also included instruments on sharing hydrological information of the Yalu Zhangbo/Brahmaputra River, which also flows through Assam in India's north-east.

China is also investing in the construction of a 6-km-long bridge across the Padma River, costing about USD 3.7 billion, and the USD 2.5 billion power plant at Payra near Dhaka. The BCIM Corridor Plan, covering a route of 2800 km, involves linking Kunming in China's Yunnan province with Kolkata, passing though nodes such as Mandalay in Myanmar and Dhaka in Bangladesh before heading to Kolkata.

The Chinese are world experts in infrastructure building; they would pay a high price for entry tickets into this space where business and politics meet. New Delhi is unlikely to formally endorse Beijing's Belt and Road Initiative, but would allow it in other forms.

Will Indian firms get a piece of BRI business cake?

The Chinese have made a mark in engineering and construction (Engineering, Procurement, Construction [EPC]), making it possible for them to build massive industrial plants and construct amazing infrastructure projects in shorter time periods and with lesser funds than Western companies.

They are now in a position to export their EPC strategy, which is really why Chinese companies have implemented major projects in foreign countries and now feel confident in assisting the government's stupendous Belt and Road Initiative. The BRI Plan, which critics describe as a geopolitical project to garner political influence, involves building connectivity infrastructure like railways and ports across more than sixty countries.

Angshu Chakraverty, managing director of Metis & Janus Ltd., an international EPC firm, cited five reasons why Chinese companies are competing successfully against Western and other competitors.

- They have a tried and tested EPC strategy.
- They can provide low-cost funds, that crucial element that can sway any project owner in a rich or poor country, because so much depends on the availability, conditions and cost of funds.
- The image of Chinese as people with a strong work ethic and a track record for completing projects in time.
- The ready availability of machinery and trained manpower ready to travel anywhere
- Quick response after a project is on offer and the bidding process begins. Western companies are often slower than the Chinese.

On the designing aspect, which is a very important element of a project, the Chinese are building their own solutions to a variety of different project needs, Chakraverty told me in an interview.

Major Chinese companies, mainly the state-owned ones, are umbrella organizations with a wide variety of subsidiaries involved in different functions. Working under one banner, it is easier for designers and engineers to pool capabilities across subsidiaries without the usual problem of ego clashes.

'I see extensive collaboration among public and private Chinese companies, among different entities pooling together solutions for funding issues, designing and procurement,' Chakraverty says. 'The scene has changed from what it was ten years ago. They are now collaborating with the Germans, the Swiss and the Norwegians as well,' he added.

Chinese companies bidding for international projects often collaborate with each other instead of competing. They may bid as cartels for geopolitical reasons. Alternatively, there may be one Chinese lead company trying to win the bidding war with foreign rivals and then outsourcing capabilities and materials from other Chinese companies. Both formats are in practise. But this does not stop China's major players from stretching out to European and American companies for collaboration or contracts on specific matters.

Can an Indian EPC find a place in China?

There is little chance of a foreign company to get an EPC contract in China but there are strong possibilities of their participating in global projects emanating from China. It's not just the difficulties in the Chinese market that are a hurdle, but also the simple fact that Indian construction and engineering companies, with few exceptions, have not advanced enough in the space of technology application and have limited experience with global projects compared to the Chinese giants.

For example, China leads in the use of robots, especially those that are enabled by artificial intelligence, deployed in large dam and bridge construction projects as well as on the factory floor. This gives them an edge in project pricing as well. This is why foreign companies including those from the US and Europe stand little chance of successfully competing with their Chinese counterparts in bagging projects under the BRI Plan. Chinese capabilities cover the entire range of EPC jobs, which include power plants, water projects, bridges, highways and railway systems.

Western companies have delivered well in water and environmental projects in countries that are sensitive to issues like environmental standards. But several markets in Asia, Africa, Latin America and Central America are more sensitive to pricing rather than high technology and environmental safety.

It's a trade-off. Governments in developing countries have to constantly ask themselves: Do they want the project done at a lower cost with a bit of collateral damage in terms of environment or give up the opportunity of raising living standards as promised by China's BRI offering?

Western EPC contractors are more successful in First World countries where the civil society is stronger than in the developing world.

'Indian companies will find it very difficult to compete with what Chinese firms can offer in terms of project financing, lower costs and project delivery expertise,' Chakraverty said.

'At the same time, if an L&T or an RIL comes in with superior technology that China doesn't have, it would love to host them. Or, if they come with cheaper credit than local loans, they would love to host them. So, look, no one is altruistic to host people for nothing and just because they like their face, definitely not,' Chakraverty said. 'If BRI is opened up in India, it is the Chinese engineering companies who will bag contracts in open bidding and not the Indian ones,' he said. The only way Indian companies can get an opportunity to learn and grow is for the government to make rules restricting the extent of FDI in project construction as China did in the initial years of reforms.

China has had its share of bad project selection and implementation in foreign countries, resulting in heavy losses. The government bore the losses without making heavy weather of it, at least in the public domain, because that would give the rulers a negative image.

When it comes to the ease of executing projects while dealing with regulators and local environmental and social groups and stakeholders, it is useful to have a state partner or a local company as a partner to soften blows and overcome challenges. This is why Chinese firms may be forced to find an Indian partner. They are mostly likely to choose the state as partner so that the state government defends them in legislations and before social groups in times of resistance.

Rebranding BRI without changing motives

China is rebranding and reworking the BRI to meet new political circumstances in the world, and address a series of complaints, some of which were flagged by the Indian government when it refused to attend its prestigious Belt and Road Forum in 2017.

Beijing started out in 2013, describing the BRI as an attempt to revive the ancient Silk Road, which evoked the travels of explorers like the Italian merchant-writer Marco Polo and the Moroccan scholar Ibn Battuta, and the exchange of tea, spices, silk, leather and other goods across land, mountain and seas through China, India and the Arab world, going as far as Turkey and beyond. It was initially called the One Belt, One Road (OBOR) programme. But it faced criticism on the ground of making the programme China-centric while claiming it was doing good to the world. Hence, 'one' was dropped to pre-empt the sense of being the only one interested. The new name is BRI.

India was the only major country to keep away from the Forum the next year, but this time it did not go public with its grievances.

Many would argue it was not wise on India's part to rub the Chinese nose in public because such acts have long-term consequences. India could have reserved its comments about the sovereignty issue instead of telling the world that it expected poor countries to fall in a debt trap if they accepted Chinese infrastructure projects.

It has often been argued that India desperately needs infrastructure development to kick-start a new economic growth cycle and China is the only source that can provide us with not just construction capabilities but also financial support at a time when funding from other world bodies including the World Bank is inadequate.

But the simple fact that escapes almost every debate is that Chinese industrial growth in the first two decades after the reforms began in 1989 was achieved with very little infrastructural support, and the awesome bridges, railways and airports that we now see were built on the money earned with exports from industries that came up in the early years.

At the BRF meeting in April 2018, China tried to overcome criticism of 'debt trap diplomacy' by agreeing to make project sustainability an important factor in judging which projects to support in foreign countries. China's finance minister, Liu Kun, said his government aimed to create a 'debt sustainability framework' to improve assessment of financial risk. He announced a new set of guidelines seeking to enhance BRI project standards and quality while requesting Chinese policy banks and international financial institutions like the World Bank, the Asian Development Bank and the European Bank for Reconstruction and Development to raise the standards of financial governance. China's Standardisation Administration followed up with a policy to enhance standards cooperation and integration with BRI countries.

The government in New Delhi is under pressure to explain Indian responses to the so-called the String of Pearls theory or belief that China is surrounding India with its connectivity projects in Pakistan, Nepal, Bangladesh, Myanmar and Sri Lanka. After its recent re-election, the Modi government said it has outlined its rebalancing strategy, highlighting its offer of soft loans for several development and capacity building projects across continents.

V. Muraleedharan, Minister of State for External Affairs, answering a query in the Lok Sabha, said that his government has a robust development cooperation agenda, constituting a significant dimension of its close and multifaceted ties with many partner countries, including in India's neighbours.

Diverse directions of the Silk Road

A significant new move by the Chinese is the emphasis on the 'digital Silk Road' concept. This is to persuade Chinese technology companies to look at opportunities in BRI countries of Asia, Africa and Latin America instead of putting all their eggs in the Western world at a time when China is facing a corrosive trade war with the US, and Europe has begun to show resistance to Chinese tech companies.

To be clear, Chinese investments in BRI projects represent just one-seventh of the country's total ODI, which is a low number that shows that developing countries are still not ready to absorb vast quantities of money from China because their economies are not strong enough and also because of fears of a debt trap.

What is equally significant is that the value of newly-signed BRI construction contracts increased by 47.7 per cent in January–March 2019, reversing a 12.8 per cent contraction in 2018, according to the *BRI Quarterly*.

'The rebound in contract values suggests that business tied to the BRI may be gathering steam again, despite past reports of project pushback. Construction contracts are highly correlated with China's overseas lending, especially in poorer countries,' it said.

The early months of 2019 saw a revival of sorts with Italy becoming the first major European country to join the BRI after formally signing a Memorandum of Understanding. This one move played a major role in softening Western criticism about BRI project sustainability, transparency and lending standards and also took some of the wind from the US sails.

The next move in April was more concrete, with the China Machinery Engineering Corporation signing a USD 135 million contract to upgrade Bulgaria's Varna Port. This is some sort of a breakthrough because it is China's first port construction job on the Black Sea.

Malaysia, which shook China by suspending a Chinese-funded railway project, changed its mind in April when the newly elected government of Prime Minister Mahathir Mohamad cancelled the Chinese-funded infrastructure project, saying it was too expensive and his country did not have enough capability to accept huge loans. One year after cancellation, Kuala Lumpur announced it was resuming work on the controversial East Coast Rail Link. Malaysia's decision to cancel the Chinese-funded project soon after the prime minister returned to power seriously hurt BRI's public image.

While the resumption helped optics for China, it was still shocked at the fact that the Malaysian government asked for a one-third reduction in costs. It had no choice but to comply. In one go, Mahathir had accomplished price reduction and proved that his election-time claims about Chinese projects being very expensive were true. Malaysia also revived the USD 34 billion China-backed Bandar Malaysia development project, which had been cancelled in 2017.

The Chinese had softened the deal by offering to build a USD 500 million artificial intelligence park in Malaysia although it would be difficult to establish a linkage between the two projects.

Very soon, the Malaysian example was picked up by other countries that began informally asking for price reduction although they did not make a public noise of it.

The Digital Silk Road will offer China an opportunity to push the businesses of its technology firms like Huawei which are facing stiff resistance in the US, Canada and other countries.

The first part of 2019 saw Huawei signing 5G-related agreements with Bahrain, Saudi Arabia and Indonesia besides launching a 5G test-bed in Thailand. What worries Huawei and Chinese authorities most is Washington's export ban, which has affected Huawei's buying of critical US-manufactured components like semiconductor devices. This ban can derail the company's growth plans. The plan can also hurt Huawei's plans on 5G rollout in these countries.

An in-depth look at Chinese motivations

Pouring into large data sets concerning China-backed infrastructure projects in different countries, the Berlin-based think tank Mercator Institute of China Studies (MERICS) pulled out four insights that would be of great value to both Indian business and the government.[5]

1. It found that investment in power plants and grids dominates Beijing's spending on BRI-related infrastructure.
2. The government in Beijing is pushing Chinese energy companies to seek contracts abroad without necessarily

prioritizing a particular segment of energy construction. It is neither leading a 'green' revolution nor a fossil-fuel revival although there are regular efforts to show BRI as some sort of heavenly gift for betterment of environment. Actually, it is playing both sides, encouraging both types of companies as long as they are able to get business abroad.

3. BRI's energy projects are geographically diversified. Latin America is in the lead in terms of volume of completed investments (mostly into renewables and energy distribution), while Southeast Asia boasts the highest number of projects (mostly involving coal).
4. The focus on energy projects creates preconditions for the next phase of the BRI plan which is industrial extension to other countries and creating China-centred supply chains.

'The BRI has been more about investing in energy than anything else,' the study said.

Nearly two-thirds of Chinese spending on completed BRI projects worth USD 50 billion have gone to the energy sector. The rest went to transport projects (more than USD 15 billion), and the Digital Silk Road (more than USD 10 billion).

Even in projects under construction, the clear emphasis is on the energy sector. They will get a similar volume of Chinese FDI and loans to projects already completed. The study said that the timetables for newer projects vary greatly, which means that some should go on-stream as early as in 2019, while others will go live only in the mid-2020s.

In other words, China is laying the ground for a massive transfer of its industrial capacity across the globe. In some ways, it is similar to global companies from Japan which use bases across many countries because their own country could neither accommodate so much capacity nor bear the high level of pollution they would generate.

There was a time when Americans saw political conspiracy in the Japanese growth-offensive, and it's now time for China to face the same criticism. This is not to say that Chinese motives are purely profit-driven. Far from it. Beijing is driving Chinese companies and directing the spread of business across strategic sectors like electricity and telecommunications because they provide it with power levers to drive its diplomatic efforts and, someday, try to overcome the overwhelming influence of the US.

The August 2019 decision separating the Ladakh region from Jammu and Kashmir, and declaring them to be two separate Union Territories under direct control of New Delhi, is also likely to impact the political dialogue on India's adoption of Belt and Road Initiation.

7

TRADING AND SLIPPING

Sweating and slipping on the trade front

Trade between China and India continues to be heavily tilted towards China in value terms while the composition highlights the shortcomings in the Make in India plan. While India's exports to China increased by 15.21 per cent and imports from China increased by a smaller 12.89 per cent in calendar year 2018, the absolute values tell the real story. India's imports from China in calendar year 2018 added up to USD 58.05 billion against exports of USD 18.83 billion, according to figures released by the Customs department of China. In other words, India buys from China triple of what it sells.

India's continuous trade deficit with China, which hit a record level in 2018, can mean one of the two things: China has been resisting Indian efforts to open up its market or Indian exporters and officials have not found a way to convince Chinese customers about the worth of their goods and services. Though there has been obvious resistance from the official level—and signals from top leaders influence decision-making by Chinese importers—it is also true that the Indian side has not been sufficiently creative and striving when it comes to finding markets in China.

India's top imports from China vary from extremely low-tech goods to those that demand high technology. The main imports include parts of mobile handsets, fully assembled mobile handsets, diodes and semiconductors, ICs, set-top boxes and storage batteries, adding up to USD 23.13 billion or 40 per cent of its imports from China.

According to the annual commercial report for calendar year 2018 released by the General Administration of Customs of China and the National Bureau of Statistics, India–China bilateral trade in 2018 increased by 13.34 per cent year-over-year (YOY) to reach USD 95.70 billion. At this rate, the bilateral trade will cross USD 100 billion in the current calendar year 2019.

In 2018, India remained the seventh-largest export destination for Chinese products. But it slipped from being lower than lowly from the position of twenty-fourth largest exporter to China in 2017 to twenty-sixth in 2018.

The trade deficit for India climbed to USD 57.86 billion in 2018 from USD 51.72 billion in 2017.

Trade in 2018

India–China bilateral trade

(in USD billion)

Year	India's exports	India's imports	Total trade	Trade deficit for India
2018	18.83	76.87	95.70	58.05
2017	16.34	68.10	84.44	51.75
% growth	15.21	12.89	13.34	12.16

Source: General Administration of Customs of China

Top five commodities

Items of India's export to China	Items of India's import from China
Organic chemicals (mainly cyclic hydrocarbons)	Parts of mobile handsets, mobile handsets, diodes and semiconductors, ICs, set-top boxes and storage batteries
Natural pearls, precious stones and precious metals (mainly diamonds)	Computers, gas compressors for ACs and fridges, ACs and parts, bearings
Cotton (cotton yarn and uncombed cotton)	Organic chemicals (hetero-cyclic compounds, antibiotics)
Copper cathodes	Plastics and articles thereof
Iron and copper ores	Optical, photographic devices, medical equipment

Source: General Administration of Customs of China

Top fifteen items of India's exports to China (two-digit HS code)

(in USD billion)

S. no.	HS code	Category	Value	% share in total import	Percentage (%) growth
	Total	**All commodity chapters**	**18.83**	**100.00**	**15.21**
1	29	Organic chemicals	2.99	15.85	72.14
2	71	Natural or cultured pearls, precious or semiprecious stones, precious metals; precious metal-clad metals, articles thereof; imitation jewellery; coin	2.90	15.41	11.10
3	52	Cotton, including yarns and woven fabrics thereof	1.61	8.53	23.94
4	74	Copper and articles thereof	1.55	8.21	-28.27

S. no.	HS code	Category	Value	% share in total import	Percentage (%) growth
	Total	**All commodity chapters**	**18.83**	**100.00**	**15.21**
5	26	Ores, slag and ash	1.40	7.46	-31.19
6	27	Mineral fuels, mineral oils and products of their distillation; bituminous substances; mineral waxes	1.13	5.98	266.87
7	25	Salt; sulphur; earths and stone; plastering materials, lime and cement	1.05	5.56	6.37
8	39	Plastics and articles thereof	1.04	5.52	137.53
9	84	Nuclear reactors, boilers, machinery and mechanical appliances; parts thereof	0.73	3.87	15.15
10	85	Electrical machinery and equipment and parts thereof; sound recorders and reproducers, television recorders and reproducers, parts and accessories	0.58	3.06	-0.19
11	15	Animal or vegetable fats and oils and their cleavage products; prepared edible fats; animal or vegetable waxes	0.42	2.22	1.95
12	03	Fish and crustaceans, molluscs and other aquatic invertebrates	0.39	2.09	231.99
13	72	Iron and steel	0.31	1.62	-35.74

S. no.	HS code	Category	Value	% share in total import	Percentage (%) growth
	Total	**All commodity chapters**	**18.83**	**100.00**	**15.21**
14	32	Tanning or dyeing extracts; tannins and derivatives; dyes, pigments and other colouring matter; paints and varnishes; putty and other mastics; inks	0.27	1.45	20.76
15	41	Raw hides and skins (other than fur skins) and leather	0.23	1.22	-9.97

Top fifteen items of India's imports from China

(in USD billion)

S. no.	HS code	Category	Value	% share in Total export	Percentage (%) growth
	Total	**All commodity chapters**	**76.87**	**100.00**	**12.89**
1	85	Electrical machinery and equipment and parts thereof; sound recorders and reproducers, television recorders and reproducers, parts and accessories	23.13	30.08	6.22

S. no.	HS code	Category	Value	% share in Total export	Percentage (%) growth
	Total	**All commodity chapters**	**76.87**	**100.00**	**12.89**
2	84	Nuclear reactors, boilers, machinery and mechanical appliances; parts thereof	13.78	17.92	13.80
3	29	Organic chemicals	8.44	10.98	28.63
4	39	Plastics and articles thereof	2.95	3.84	10.10
5	90	Optical, photographic, cinematographic, measuring, checking, precision, medical or surgical instruments and apparatus; parts and accessories thereof	1.95	2.54	6.97
6	73	Articles of iron or steel	1.86	2.42	26.28
7	94	Furniture; bedding, cushions etc.; lamps and lighting fittings nesoi; illuminated signs, nameplates and the like; prefabricated buildings	1.64	2.13	-3.96
8	87	Vehicles, other than railway or tramway rolling stock, and parts and accessories thereof	1.63	2.11	27.17
9	31	Fertilizers	1.57	2.04	52.03

S. no.	HS code	Category	Value	% share in Total export	Percentage (%) growth
	Total	**All commodity chapters**	**76.87**	**100.00**	**12.89**
10	72	Iron and steel	1.49	1.94	-1.35
11	95	Toys, games and sports equipment; parts and accessories thereof	1.06	1.38	62.00
12	76	Aluminium and articles thereof	1.05	1.36	51.26
13	27	Mineral fuels, mineral oils and products of their distillation; bituminous substances; mineral waxes	1.00	1.30	40.32
14	28	Inorganic chemicals; organic or inorganic compounds of precious metals, of rare-earth metals, of radioactive elements or of isotopes	0.97	1.26	78.03
15	70	Glass and glassware	0.83	1.08	12.35

Top five competitors of the top fifteen of India's exports to China

(in USD billion)

HS code	Category	Competitors	Value	% share in total Import
	Total	**World**	**67.43**	**100.00**
29	**Organic chemicals**	Korea South	14.11	20.92
		Saudi Arabia	7.46	11.06
		Japan	7.42	11.00
		Taiwan	6.72	9.96
		United States	3.86	5.72
	Total	**World**	**61.89**	**100**
71	**Natural or cultured pearls, precious or semiprecious stones, precious metals**	Switzerland	18.50	29.89
		South Africa	13.51	21.82
		Australia	8.25	13.33
		Canada	4.60	7.43
		United States	3.24	5.23
	Total	**World**	**9.89**	**100.00**
52	**Cotton, including yarn and woven fabric thereof**	Vietnam	2.22	22.46
		India	1.61	16.23
		United States	1.11	11.18
		Pakistan	0.95	9.61
		Australia	0.90	9.12
	Total	**World**	**47.66**	**100.00**
74	**Copper and articles thereof**	Chile	10.18	21.36
		Zambia	3.86	8.11
		Japan	3.74	7.85
		Taiwan	2.53	5.30
		Korea South	2.26	4.74

HS code	Category	Competitors	Value	% share in total Import
	Total	**World**	**67.43**	**100.00**
	Total	**World**	**135.78**	**100.00**
26	**Ores, slag and ash**	Australia	52.24	38.47
		Brazil	19.10	14.07
		Peru	11.74	8.64
		Chile	10.85	7.99
		South Africa	8.11	5.98
	Total	**World**	**347.28**	**100.00**
27	**Mineral fuel, oil etc.; bitumen substitute mineral; wax**	Russia	42.03	12.10
		Saudi Arabia	31.30	9.01
		Angola	25.45	7.33
		Australia	22.83	6.57
		Iraq	22.45	6.46
	Total	**World**	**8.02**	**100.00**
25	**Salt; sulphur; earths and stone; lime and cement plaster**	Australia	1.38	17.22
		India	1.05	13.05
		Turkey	0.96	12.02
		Vietnam	0.56	7.03
		United States	0.41	5.10
	Total	**World**	**74.87**	**100.00**
39	**Plastics and articles thereof**	Korea South	11.70	15.63
		Japan	9.82	13.11
		Taiwan	9.69	12.95
		United States	7.08	9.46
		Saudi Arabia	5.98	7.98
	Total	**World**	**202.27**	**100.00**

HS code	Category	Competitors	Value	% share in total Import
	Total	**World**	**67.43**	**100.00**
84	**Nuclear reactors, boilers, machinery etc.; parts thereof**	Japan	40.70	20.12
		Germany	24.00	11.87
		Korea South	23.77	11.75
		United States	18.27	9.03
		Taiwan	14.89	7.36
	Total	**World**	**521.98**	**100.00**
85	**Electrical machinery etc., sound equipment; TV equipment; PTS**	Taiwan	113.50	21.74
		Korea South	100	19.16
		Japan	44.44	8.51
		Vietnam	34.11	6.54
		Malaysia	33.96	6.51
	Total	**World**	**8.62**	**100**
15	**Animal or vegetable fats and oils and their cleavage products**	Indonesia	3.53	41.02
		Malaysia	1.42	16.46
		Canada	0.95	11.02
		Ukraine	0.44	5.16
		India	0.42	4.86
	Total	**World**	**11.61**	**100**
03	**Fish and crustaceans, molluscs and other aquatic invertebrates**	Russia	2.11	18.20
		United States	1.25	10.78
		Canada	1.00	8.65
		Australia	0.63	5.46
		Norway	0.58	4.99

HS code	Category	Competitors	Value	% share in total Import
	Total	**World**	**67.43**	**100.00**
	Total	**World**	**22.38**	**100.00**
72	**Iron and steel**	Japan	5.70	25.46
		Korea South	3.54	15.81
		Indonesia	2.93	13.08
		Taiwan	1.42	6.35
		South Africa	1.39	6.21
	Total	**World**	**5.03**	**100.00**
32	**Tanning and dye ext etc.; dye, paint, putty etc.; inks**	Japan	1.12	22.24
		Germany	0.64	12.79
		Korea South	0.60	11.84
		United States	0.51	10.07
		Taiwan	0.46	9.10
	Total	**World**	**4.78**	**100.00**
41	**Raw hides and skins (no fur skins) and leather**	United States	0.89	18.54
		Brazil	0.53	11.10
		Italy	0.47	9.91
		Australia	0.44	9.25
		India	0.23	4.81

Source for all above charts: General Administration of Customs of China

Indian ambassador to China, Vikram Misri, announced in early June 2019 that the bilateral trade between the two countries will reach USD 100 billion in 2019. This was the target set by Chinese President Xi Jinping and Indian Prime Minister Narendra Modi in 2015.

'The economic and commercial engagement between India and China constitutes a major component of our bilateral relations. Last year, our bilateral trade crossed USD 95 billion and we expect it to cross the USD 100 billion mark in the near future,' Misri said while inaugurating a new factory launched by Kochi-based Synthite Industries at Wucheng County in eastern China's Shandong province.[1]

'Chinese companies like Xiaomi, Haier, Oppo, etc., have become household names in India. I am also proud to inform that there are around 125 Indian companies operating in Mainland China in various sectors like information technology, manufacturing, textiles, food processing, etc.,' Misri said at the Synthite inauguration event.

He described Synthite as 'one of the leading enterprises from India to foray into Mainland China with its first investment in Xinjiang in 2012.' Lauding the Indian company's efforts, the ambassador said, 'Their professionalism, combined with diligent planning, has helped them forge ahead despite early setbacks.'

The company, which was represented by its managing director Viju Jacob at the event, has invested USD 50 million in three different plants in China. It plans to meet requirements for extracts of Indian chilly, curry leaves, black pepper, ginger, garlic and Chinese sweet paprika in both the Chinese and international markets.

Are we playing the trade card smartly?

We have spent years trying to persuade China to buy more and expand its basket of imports from India to include a variety of items including agriculture goods and certain grains. We have also complained about the Chinese bureaucracy responding very slowly and sometimes being indifferent.

But chest thumping won't take us far unless we examine what can be done to improve our ability to sell in the international market. There is a huge untapped potential that Indian government and exporters can tap if the right conditions are created. Much of it is improving conditions at home and not in the international market.

'There are approximately 2690 products in which India has untapped export potential to China,' Prabir De, professor and coordinator of ASEAN-India Centre at the Research and Information System for Developing Countries (RIS), told me in an interview.

The potential is more than 30 per cent in several items of export, which include rice, horticulture products, cotton and cotton textiles, garments, bovine meat, jewellery and chemical products.

The reverse is also true. India can drastically reduce its import bill by discouraging some extremely low-technology goods that could include things like hairpins, idols of gods and simple electrical and kitchen appliances. Small and medium industry either makes these goods in small numbers or have stopped manufacturing because imports are cheaper and hassle-free.

De says it is more a demand-and-supply story. Chinese goods have grown in demand in India even as the local market expanded in size in recent years. 'With dismantling border barriers, China moved fast in Indian markets with all kind of goods—low-value to high-value,' he said.

What must not be overlooked is the fact that Chinese imports have helped India expand its global exports. India could export many new products and services too, which are embedded with Chinese products. A great example is RPG's Saregama musical radio, he said.

'Yes, there are social and political implications. There are issues like job losses and security threats,' he said. The answer lies in foreign direct investments from China to India. Increased Chinese FDI will help India to raise its export portfolio,' he added.

New Delhi is in the middle of a critical balancing act. There is a need to raise duty on certain products to encourage Chinese companies to invest in manufacturing in India instead of sending the goods made in China. Recent years have seen Chinese companies establishing production units for products like mobile phones and other goods because the Indian government made it costlier to import from China.

But New Delhi is also under international pressure to reduce tariffs and possibly enter into a trade agreement with China.

'Increasing tariffs wouldn't help Indian production as most of the country's export sector depends very much on imported parts and components. I think de-escalation of trade war, particularly between US and China, will restore the globalization,' De said.

An interesting question is whether it is time for India to insist on binding ratios instead of merely setting overall target for bilateral trade. For instance, China could be asked to make assurances about expanding its purchase basket to include some specific Indian goods, and buy at least 40 per cent of the value of total trade.

'I don't agree. When we trust the system of free trade, quota is not the solution,' De said, adding, 'What we need between India and China is a gradual opening of trade.'

He added that India and China should go for a Partial Trade Area (PTA) agreement instead of a full-scale Free Trade Area agreement. A PTA will make it possible for India and China to exchange goods among themselves with favourable terms as in a trade bloc. 'A stronger trade relation between India and China is needed to drive the global trade,' he said.

On the other hand, some of the principles of free trade have been trampled in the midst of a trade war between the world's largest and second-largest economies, and smaller trade players like India need not remain stuck to the old rules of the game. It's time to seek opportunities.

Some would ask if China would have remained confined to the rules of free trade if it was at the losing end of the trade competition. Beijing may have asked for guarantees from its trade partners about how much Chinese goods would be bought. It is already linking some of its diplomatic moves with assurances of higher buying of Chinese goods from different countries.

Trade pattern

The expectation of crossing the USD 100 billion mark comes from the performance of 2018 when bilateral trade came to USD 95.54 billion. But there was a decline of 3.59 per cent in the total trade as compared to the first five months of 2018. This dented optimism that the total trade volume may cross USD 100 billion mark in 2019.

The bilateral trade in the first five months of 2019 was USD 36.87 billion. The composition of the bilateral trade says it all: India sells raw materials to China and buys manufactured products (read value-addition). According to China's data, in 2018, organic chemicals became India's number one export commodity to China, surpassing exports of natural stones like diamonds. India's top exports to China included organic chemicals (mainly cyclic hydrocarbons), diamonds, cotton yarn, pure copper and iron ore. Besides, export of Indian agricultural-animal products (HSC1-24) to China increased by 41 per cent to reach USD 1.01 billion in 2018 from USD 750 million in 2017. The main products of exports were marine products, castor oil, dried and shelled leguminous vegetables, dried capsicum, tea, fruits, fruit jams, medicinal plants, guar gum, sugar, sesame seeds, vegetable seeds, cotton lint, grapes etc. On the other hand, Chinese export of agricultural-animal products decreased by 22 per cent to reach USD 340 million in 2018.

For India, the focus is on growing its exports of agriculture-animal products, including rice, sugar, oil meal, tea, grapes, mangoes and marine products, and it has to build on the successful buyer–seller meets organized throughout 2018. Pharmaceuticals would also remain a focus in the coming years.

China's top exports to India included electrical machinery and equipment, machinery and mechanical equipment, organic chemicals, plastics, fertilizers and antibiotics. Its total trade with the world increased by 13.05 per cent in 2018 YOY to USD 4.6 trillion—imports increased by 17.82 per cent to USD 2.11 trillion while its exports increased by 9.31 per cent to USD 2.49 trillion. China, thus, had a trade surplus of USD 382.38 billion with YOY decrease of 21.83 per cent. The top five export destinations for Chinese products were the US, Hong Kong, Japan, South Korea and Vietnam. The top five exporters to China, on the other hand, were South Korea, Japan, Taiwan, the US and Germany.

In 2018, India's export of organic chemicals to China surpassed the export of diamonds, which was the number one commodity the previous year. Chapter-wise, India's top exports to China included organic chemicals (mainly cyclic hydrocarbons), diamonds, cotton, copper, iron ore, mineral fuels and oils, granite, salt, sulphur and plastic polymers.

India exports of organic chemicals grew 72.14 per cent to USD 2.99 billion. In the last two years, export of organic chemicals to China has tripled. There has been significant growth in export of cyclic hydrocarbons such as paraxylene (1, 4-dimethylbenzene) (HS code 290243) and benzene (HSC290220); menthol (HSC290611), ethylene glycol (HSC290531) and ethylene or ethene (HSC290121). India was the second-largest exporter of diamonds (mainly non-industrial grade) to China, with a share of 32.22 per cent (USD 2.86 billion).

India's cotton (mainly cotton yarn and uncombed cotton) exports to China increased by 23.94 per cent to USD 1.61 billion. India was the second-largest exporter of cotton to China with a 16.23 per cent market share, just after Vietnam. Indian exports of copper (mostly cathodes) and iron ore registered a negative growth of 28.27 per cent and 31.19 per cent respectively to USD 1.55 billion and USD 1.40 billion. Export of mineral fuels and oils (mainly naphtha and diesel oils) grew by 266.87 per cent. India was the largest exporter of granite stone, salt and mica to China, with shares of 68 per cent, 58 per cent and 76 per cent respectively. Export of salt grew by 29 per cent YOY. India's granite export was USD 679 million, salt USD 209 million and mica USD 59 million.

India's export of plastic articles, mainly polymers of ethylene and propylene, showed robust growth of 138 per cent and reached USD 1.04 billion. India exported diesel engines, taps and valves worth USD 113 million, registering an increase of 27 per cent and 39 per cent respectively. India exported electronic machinery equipment, mostly static converters, switching apparatus to China to the value of USD 577 million. With a market share of 99 per cent, India is the largest supplier of castor oil to China, valued at USD 384 million. Indian export of fishery products, mostly shrimps, prawn and frozen fish grew by 232 per cent YOY to reach USD 393 million. India's export of frozen fish grew by 1200 per cent, from USD 9 million in 2017 to USD 120 million in 2018.

China's exports to India

In 2018, China's exports of electrical machinery and equipment (HSC85) to India increased by a little over 6 per cent to USD 23.13 billion (mainly parts of mobiles, mobile handsets, diodes and semiconductors, ICs, set-top boxes, storage batteries, transformers, TV cameras etc.).

Chinese export of machinery and mechanical equipment (HSC84) (mainly computers, refrigeration compressors, ball bearings, printers, taps/cocks/valves, parts of heavy machinery etc.) saw an increase of 13.80 per cent to USD 13.76 billion. India was the second-largest export destination for Chinese organic chemicals, growing 29 per cent YOY worth to reach USD 898 million in 2018, with a share of 25.76 per cent. Chinese export of plastics increased by 10 per cent to reach USD 2.95 billion.

India was the largest export destination of fertilizers exports from China to the value of USD 1.57 billion, growing 22.32 per cent YOY. The fertilizers included mainly ammonium phosphate (85 per cent) and urea (13 per cent) to India. Chinese export of ammonium phosphate to India grew by 76 per cent YOY to reach USD 1.3 billion in value terms and 45 per cent in quantity to reach 3.2 million tonnes.

The list of top five commodities exported by India to China illustrates why India is losing in the value game. The top two items that India imported from China in 2018 were parts of mobile handsets, mobile handsets, diodes and semiconductors, ICs, set-top boxes and storage batteries (adding up to USD 23.13 billion), followed by nuclear reactors, boilers, machinery and mechanical appliances; parts thereof (USD 13.78 billion). After this, the values on the import list peter down to single digits.

On the investment front, China put a total of 4.75 billion in India till December 2017. During calendar year 2017, it had invested USD 289.98 million. On the other hand, India's cumulative investment in China up to December 2017 was USD 854 million. In calendar year 2017, India invested USD 158 million in China.

Meanwhile, China's total outward FDI flows in calendar year 2018 added up to USD 129.83 billion, a growth of 4.2 per cent YOY, while China attracted FDI worth USD 134.97 billion in 2018.

Door opening for Indian pharma firms

An area that holds great potential for Indian exports and involvement of Indian companies in China is the pharmaceutical industry. China has given several indications that it is about to open up the sector to usher in a huge quantity of Indian drugs in the local market. The demand in China is massive.

There is an expectation of more than a thirty-fold increase in the export of Indian drugs to around USD 1 billion in just about two years if doors are opened up. Indian exports are now languishing at USD 30 million a year.

Even at a USD 1 billion level, China's import of Indian drugs would be just about 5 per cent of India's drug export of USD 19 billion. 'There's really no limit. Indian exports can go up to USD 5 billion if regulatory obstacles are removed and Indian drugs are allowed in freely,' a pharmaceutical industry executive told me.

Take anti-cancer drugs. About 4.3 million new cancer patients are diagnosed in China every year. Very few domestic companies produce self-developed anti-cancer drugs. China imported USD 7 billion worth of this kind of drugs until 2018.

Since India is possibly the cheapest source capable of providing quality anti-cancer drugs at half or less than half the price charged by Western companies, it can quickly get a significant share of this import. Even a 10 per cent share of this import bill on anti-cancer drugs can expand India's exports by USD 700 million. Many think a 20 per cent share in this category of drugs is eminently possible for India.

Contrast this with the fact that total drug purchase from India is USD 30 million and a clear picture would emerge. What is crucial is the door-opening move from Beijing because it is a win-win proposition for both countries. India specializes in generic medicines prepared after processing, while China is one of the world's biggest suppliers of active pharmaceutical ingredients (APIs), which is the molecule that does the actual work.

China desperately needs low-cost medicines to combat cancer, tuberculosis and a variety of other diseases, and India may be the only source that can provide them at prices affordable to the general public. Chinese film censors even allowed the screening of a movie *Dying to Survive*, which depicted large-scale smuggling of cancer drugs from India with patients and their family members justifying the law-breaking because the government has left them with no option in the face of an unaffordable drug market. This was a rare occasion when the Communist Party allowed criticism of government policy on the silver screen apparently after gauging the rising anger in China over high-cost medicines.

But persuading health ministry officials to closely look at the regulatory barriers that are stopping Indian drugs from flowing into China is a different ball game. It has not been easy for the Indian Embassy in Beijing, which has been battling for years to be persuasive enough to present the case of the Indian pharmaceutical industry to local regulatory officials.

The Indian side had been waiting for precisely this sort of meeting for years until it finally happened in June 2019. The delay was not a coincidence, nor was the timing of the meeting ahead of the scheduled visit of Chinese President Xi Jinping to New Delhi in October 2019.

Officials and pharmaceutical industry executives from India sat down with Chinese officials to explain their point of view, understand why Beijing has been reluctant to allow wide market access to India-made medicines and find ways to resolve the challenge.

The meeting, which took place in Shanghai, involved India's drug regulator S.E. Reddy and the Deputy Commissioner of China's National Medical Products Administration Xu Jinghe, besides other officials and representatives of the pharmaceutical industry in both countries. Reddy stressed the need for the Chinese regulator to play a bigger role as a facilitator for importing low-cost drugs that were affordable to ordinary Chinese citizens. The Indian Embassy's economic officer Prashant Lokhande suggested that China's provincial governments cooperate with Indian authorities to facilitate the speedy registration and procurement process for Indian medicines.

Another Indian official, Anil Rai, India's Consul General in Shanghai, touched on several issues that are hurdles for Indian firms, such as registration, regulator's vetting of drugs before granting permission and regulatory inspections and compliance. At the meeting, which was attended by representatives of thirty-five Indian pharmaceutical companies and thirty such companies from China, Xu said he looked forward to further engagement with Indian authorities to sort out issues connected to import of medicines from India.

A report[2] of the meeting in the Chinese official media said the meeting signals that generic drugs produced in India may soon enjoy better access to the Chinese market. It was attended by officials of China's National Medical Product Administration (NMPA) and Indian regulators. It covered issues concerning generic drug research and development (R&D), manufacturing, and regulatory supervision.

Reports listed some issues that were discussed as follows:

- legislation, policy regulation and technical specifications on licensing import drugs
- compliance guidelines for pharma exports
- China's drug procurement policies and procedures

- Sino-India pharma R&D collaboration
- registration and licensing of APIs

Chinese regulators are especially concerned with ensuring these drugs are of good quality and affordable, the official media said. NMPA pledged to institutionalize bioequivalence (BE) testing requirements for India-made low-cost generics. The report quoted an anonymous industry insider suggesting that Indian generic companies are also eager to join the bid, offering to cut prices by 20 to 30 per cent from the bid level.

There are signs that Chinese regulators did some tough negotiations, leveraging India's strong need for selling drugs. In negotiations with Chinese, it is essential not to expose one's vulnerabilities and to work on the weaknesses of the other side, which in the case of China is the crying need for low-cost drugs for which it cannot find a better source.

Chinese media also pointed out that recent regulatory changes in the US market have affected sales of Indian generics. This is why enhanced drug exports to China is crucial to Indian drug makers. India's share in the global drug market is 3.6 per cent, and it plans to raise it to seven per cent by 2030. This will require a 10–11 per cent increase in India's pharmaceutical production, according to a report by the Indian Pharmaceutical Association and consultant McKinsey.

Did India negotiate hard enough to extract concessions from the Chinese officials? This will be known in the coming months when Beijing is expected to come out with new rules relaxing drug exports from India.

A few Indian companies have already launched testing and production in China. They include an initial USD 16 million investment made Aurovitas Pharma (Taizhou) Ltd in July 2018. The end of 2018 saw another deal between Shandong Luoxin Pharmaceutical Co Ltd and Aurobindo Pharma to produce airway and respiratory devices. According to the Chinese media, early 2019 witnessed Dr Reddy Laboratories Ltd's BE test application for its clopidogrel hydrogen sulphate tablets.

In the end, it will require a lot of political pressure from New Delhi and some give and take before Beijing shows a higher level of generosity than its present attitude of bit-by-bit opening. European and American companies face similar resistance, but they have greater patience and deeper pockets to battle it out in the Chinese market.

Cracks in the door

China announced in late August 2019 that it will show greater leniency for import of small quantities of generic drugs, which are not approved by Chinese health authorities but sold legally in other countries. Such medicines, brought in small quantities, will no more be classified as 'fake medicines'.

In effect, it opens the doors for free movement of Indian drugs as long as they are bought by individual patients and their relatives. Such acts were earlier described as smuggling. Beijing-based *Global Times* indicated that even bulk imports of these drugs may be allowed as long as the importer obtains a licence.

'People who want to import generic drugs for profit still have to follow Chinese laws to register and get an approval in advance,' the paper quoted Liu Changgiu, a health law expert and researcher at the Shanghai Academy of Social Sciences, as saying.[3]

Imported drugs are costly in China because of high tariffs, multiple layers of distribution, and monopoly supply in certain types of medicines. Imported anticancer medications usually cost double or triple in China as compared to other markets. In some case, they are four to five times costlier for the end consumer.

Huge numbers of Chinese patients respond simply by giving up treatment because they do not want to take away savings meant for all members of the family. Other seek solutions in smuggled drugs that mostly come from India.

China took a big step to remedy the problem on 1 May 2018, when it eliminated the tariff on twenty-eight categories of imported drugs to push down their prices. Some would ask why a relatively prosperous government did not make this sacrifice in tax revenue earlier. Besides bringing down import duty to zero, Beijing cut value-added tax for imported anti-cancer drugs, including 103 preparations and fifty-one raw materials, from the original 17 per cent to a mere 3 per cent.

Earlier, the tariff on imported drugs was about 5–6 per cent. By eliminating the taxes, patients made a saving of USD 312 million.

The total market value of current Chinese anticancer drugs is around USD 22 billion; imported drugs contribute about one-third. Thus, it is estimated that removing the tariff can help to save approximately USD 312 million annually for Chinese patients.

Indian companies must share a part of the blame for low sales of their drugs in China. The approval process in China is an extremely long one, and foreign importers must both deposit high sums of money and provide elaborate clinical reports before obtaining permission to sell their products. They have shown reluctance to spend time and money because their focus is on a short period.

Time may be slipping out of their hands, and they need to act quickly. China's generic drug sector is growing, with drug companies investing heavily in research and development in the hope of developing their intellectual property. Chinese scientists in the pharmaceutical sector are being paid as much as the salaries of American scientists to stop the brain drain and encourage overseas Chinese scientists to return home.

'China is at a critical stage, as it moves towards its ultimate goal of transforming from a generics to an originators superpower. New drugs spend a lot of time in R&D, bear high economic risks, often require large investments and can be easily copied,' the European Chamber of Commerce in China said in a position paper on the healthcare business in the country.

Also, 'Without sufficient IP protection, there is a high chance that there will be less of a return on investment, which creates difficulties for decision-makers and may demotivate pharmaceutical companies from innovating further. Strengthening IP protection is, therefore, essentially the only way to successfully encourage the development of innovative drugs,' it said.

The most significant advantage for the zero-tariff regime would be to suppliers of generic drugs, which most Indian companies are doing. There is a slow change from the earlier system when tariff and the slow approval process of drug authorities for imported drugs had protected local manufacturers. Now, the government is listening to the needs for low-cost drugs more than the need to protect and facilitate the growth of domestic companies.

Indian drug makers must welcome one more move by the Chinese government. In April 2018, China's State Council announced new steps for reducing the price of imported drugs in ways that can help Indian exporters. The government said it would be accelerating the import and listing of innovative medications, strengthening the intellectual property protection and improving quality control and supervision.

'On the basis of lowering the tax rate, we will also apply a number of steps to improve the supply of anticancer drugs, including centralized procurement, medical insurance payment, rational drug administration, R&D, etc.,' said Yixin Zeng, deputy director of China's Health Committee. 'Foreseeably, with their implementation one after one, these policies will work together and create a synergy effect, paving the way for deepening the structural reform of medicine supply and stimulating the market vitality. Eventually, this will help to reduce the heavy burden on China's cancer patients,' he further said.

A reduced tariff would mean lower-priced drugs and an expansion of the market for imported drugs in China. This can be of huge advantage for Indian companies who do not have enough resources to spend on marketing and communicating with hundreds of government hospitals scattered around this vast country.

As we have seen earlier, the official Chinese media report of the Shanghai meeting clearly stated that China's drug authorities want

Indian companies to share the research and development work with Chinese companies.

This is the second bottleneck relating to IPR. Indian companies are reluctant to share know-how because that would allow Chinese companies to climb up the food chain in the drug research field, and ultimately push away those very Indian companies which had shared R&D in the first place in the international market.

China also holds the key in being one of the biggest producers of basic chemicals or APIs that goes in the making of medicines and access to processing knowledge can complete the chain. It's to be expected that Chinese companies would seize the advantage in this lucrative market if they managed to take the crucial know-how from Indian drug makers what Western companies have refused to share for decades.

Why India?

'So why has India become the world's pharmacy?' asked Chen Zuobing, vice president of Zhejiang University Hospital and director of Kangfu Medical Center at Peking University Third Hospital, in an article published in Caixin website.

'India produces huge volumes of cheap generic drugs a year. Not only do these drugs have huge appeal for customers in developing countries, but they are also popular in the US, Europe and Japan, with close to 40 per cent of generic drugs in the American market originating in India,' Chen said.[4]

'India's status in the generic-drug industry also stems from its unique laws: It refuses to register pharmaceutical patents, and allows local manufacturers to produce generic versions of foreign drugs,' he said.

Although some people in India may question this simplified explanation of a complicated situation, Indian laws allow local businesses to apply for generic-drug production permits from the Indian government in cases where it is hard to obtain or pay for foreign versions of a drug. 'As a consequence, India's generic-drug industry was able to grow rapidly,' he said while advocating the broader use of generic drugs because they are more affordable to the poor.

'But could fewer protections for pharmaceutical patents hamper innovation in the industry? This is the question that has hovered over India's pharmaceutical patent system for decades, resulting in numerous lawsuits,' he said.

A vast market awaits Indian drug makers

It is essential for Indian businesses to look at China's health industry closely. Over three decades of the one-child policy and consistent rise in the standard of living have resulted in a keen awareness for leading a healthy and disease-free life and a massive demand for high levels of medical facilities. This is what has led to the government unveiling its Healthy China 2030 programme.

Having realized the importance of foreign partners in its endeavour for improvement of health standards, the government has expressed its seriousness by making the process of registration of newcomers more efficient, improved market supervision and tried to align Chinese laws and regulations with international norms. Efficiencies have also been infused in areas like protection of intellectual property (IP) enforcement, which is a sore point with foreign players. A big step is towards a regime of transparent pricing and reimbursement to encourage international companies to bring innovative drugs to the Chinese market.

In China, life expectancy and the people's overall level of health has reached the levels of middle- to high-income countries. At the same time, China is facing challenges similar to those faced by developed countries in the West.

It's a paradox because China still has a very low per capita income, but it is faced with challenges like an ageing population. Seniors often have several chronic diseases, some of which are expensive to treat. The country's healthcare expenses have been growing at a double-digit annual rate for the past decade. This has been a matter of serious grievances which are openly aired across China and also acknowledged by authorities.

The National People's Congress (NPC), which is the Chinese Parliament, decided in 2018 to restructure the ministries and commissions responsible for public health. The former National Health and Family Planning Commission (NHFPC) became the National Health Commission (NHC), and the China Food and Drug Administration (CFDA) was transformed into the China National Drug Administration (CNDA) under the State Administration for Market Regulation (SAMR).

The purpose of the restructuring was to consolidate government resources and avoid duplication of tasks by different agencies. The goal is to enhance efficiencies in health services and cut down the costs, which is overbearing for a large section of the citizens.

China has taken a series of measures to reduce the burden of high prices of drugs on patients. One of the decisions made in 2017 involved ordering hospitals not to charge a mark-up price on the drugs they give to their patients after outsourcing them. The idea was to stop the practice of charging high amounts for medicines and overmedicating patients.

8

PUBLIC DISCOURSES: A CRUCIAL CHALLENGE

China is going beyond the drive to become an economic power. It wants worldwide influence over the public discourse through the media including the Internet media, which is another area where it is challenging American dominance.

India must take note of this fact and watch how Chinese funded online news media in booming in the country because there are no government controls on foreign investments in the online media business. Politicians, media barons and journalists have fought pitched battles over whether respected international media brands like the *Financial Times* and *Washington Post* should be allowed to enter with majority stakes in local companies and the very same people did not notice the quiet entry of Chinese investments in the Internet-driven news media. Ironic, isn't it?

The ruling Communist Party of China regards propaganda, and hence the media, as an essential tool to take forward its agenda not just within the country but in the international arena as well.

'Discourse power is a pillar of the nation. Discourse is indispensable to the revival of a great nation,' wrote He Yiting executive vice president of the Central Party School, in a Communist Party paper, *Study Times*, in 2017.[1]

'China is a giant on the move, and it will ultimately become a powerhouse of discourse too,' he wrote. 'The "rejuvenation of

Chinese discourse" will come hand-in-hand with what Chinese President Xi Jinping has called "the great rejuvenation of the Chinese nation",' he said.

These are not thoughts coming from an individual but reflect the combined resolve of the ruling party in China.

It is difficult to find a clear strategy of the Indian government in the area of international discourse, which is essential for successful diplomacy. The near-absence of a strategy leaves the field clear for individual political activists like some from the RSS and members of certain think tanks to speak about India's role in the world, although they may not reflect the combined viewpoint of the Indian government.

Indian missions and consulates do little to put forth the country's point of view on international issues except for giving a few interviews to the local media of the foreign country in which they are located. Usually, a junior Indian Foreign Service official is given the task of coordination with the media.

During the seventy-five-day border dispute between Indian and Chinese troops in Doklam on the Sikkim border, which ended in August 2017, the Indian Embassy in Beijing had nothing to share with Indian journalists based in Beijing. The five correspondents representing the Indian media had little option other than putting out viewpoints expressed on a daily basis by the Ministry of Foreign Affairs in Beijing because Indian envoys were not even available for background briefing. The Embassy really is not to blame because media policy is controlled from New Delhi, which is more anxious to control the narrative than use it to India's advantage.

Successive Indian ambassadors in Beijing routinely meet Beijing-based Indian journalists on an off-the-record basis although they speak on record with the local media in China. The government could have taken advantage of the presence of the Indian media in Beijing to more effectively articulate its viewpoints on India–China relations but has let the opportunity pass. The Ministry of External

Affairs is doing itself no favour by disallowing the ambassador—the man on the ground—to speak formally to Indian journalists stationed in Beijing, although he speaks on record with the Chinese media. There is a need to share with them New Delhi's perception of difference to ensure proper reporting from Beijing, instead of reporting the Chinese version supplied by the Ministry of Foreign Affairs in Beijing.

How image affects business

An important reason for holding back Indian investments in China and vice versa is the negative media coverage of each other in the two countries. Companies such as Huawei have suffered government action after news stories emerged in Western countries and India that its telecommunication equipment contains embedded software that could allow the Chinese authorities to monitor and report user activity.

Investors see the cacophony heard in business and political meetings over the formal and social media as serious political risks.

The relationship between the Himalayan neighbours has gone up and down since the 1962 war and often taken deep dives for a variety of reasons, which are:

- Indians, more so the Indian media, thinks that China is not being a friend by backing Pakistan with not just arms and economic capability but with international prestige and shielding it from world opinion on the issue of terrorism. China for years blocked a committee of the United Nations Security Council from declaring Masood Azhar, the leader of a banned terror group, as an international terrorist. Beijing finally relented to Indian pressure for lifting its objection but not before the Pulwama strike by terrorists that killed forty Indian soldiers and led to further besmirching of China's reputation as a supporter of Pakistan in the eyes of Indians.

- China is worried about the possible reincarnation of the Dalai Lama if the earthly life of the incumbent, regarded as a living god by Tibetans, comes to an end. There are fears that the reincarnation might take place among Tibetans settled in India, or worse for China, among those living in the US. That would seriously complicate matters for Beijing. It has already come out with laws to control the reincarnation process and made sure that the child chosen by Communist authorities is selected as the next living god. It wants Indian support in gaining approval of the new incarnation because a green signal from India would go a long way for Beijing to convince millions of Tibetans about the genuineness of the choice. Will India do this favour, and for what?
- China thinks India is not only sheltering, but it is also giving political encouragement to the Dalai Lama, the leader of Tibetans, who fled from his homeland and settled in India in 1952. It has pressured many countries to deny a visa to the Dalai Lama to limit his lecturing tours across the world, which has been going on for decades. Today, the Tibetan leader has become the spiritual guru of many Westerners and Beijing's Communist leaders are worried that some of his international influence is rubbing on elite Chinese who travel across the world. New Delhi has been cautious, often knocking down signs of Tibetan protests against Chinese authorities on Indian soil, to ensure Beijing's suspicions against India do not grow.
- There are regular controversies in India over issues like China blocking it from joining international organizations such as the Nuclear Suppliers's Group until China's ally Pakistan gets a seat in it. China waited for years for Pakistan to be ready to join the Shanghai Cooperation Organization until it agreed to invite India. Of course, India's joining the SCO did widen the influence of SCO, but Beijing would want to make sure Pakistan was there to defend itself from

any possible charges of encouraging cross-border terrorism. China is also not eager to see India get a permanent seat on the United Nations Security Council.

- China's state-run media has been as active in sprinkling vitriol towards India as the Indian media is towards China. Security issues are prominent in their minds. At one stage, Mandarin-language newspaper *Lianhe Zaobao* said that Chinese military exercises are meant to 'strike awe in India'.[2] The Beijing-based *Global Times* is watched closely by Indian diplomats because it is extremely critical of India for long stretches but suddenly softens once in a while when Chinese President Xi Jinping makes friendly gestures towards India.
- Media on both sides have celebrated the informal meeting between Prime Minister Modi and President Xi in the Chinese city of Wuhan in 2018. The idea was to get to know each other by talking without aides and being burdened by thoughts of people who may already be biased. The meeting, which took place shortly after the border stand-off between the two countries at Doklam, is regarded as a positive turning point in the relationship. These and many such issues cloud the atmosphere although there is some truth and some exaggeration in all the charges and counter-charges levelled against each other in the two countries.

But why have Chinese companies like Haier and mobile brands like Xiaomi managed to penetrate deep into consumer minds in India?

Image guru Dilip Cherian has some interesting thoughts about China's image in India. 'The negative image of China in India is clearly played up by Indian media. There is a segment of the administrative and military apparatus who recognize that China is one of India's two big threats, the other obvious one being Pakistan,' he said.

On the business side, China's image has been damaged for another reason.

'The negative image of China, if one looks beyond the dominant security aspect, is that Chinese companies seem to have hurt a lot of Indian manufacturers. When you combine the potential defence vulnerabilities with the business damage, the resultant image is of an invasive and dangerous neighbour. Not a very comfortable investor or investment destination,' he said.

But then, Chinese mobile phone makers cut through the negative image and came out in the lead. Clearly, a negative image in India is not so long-lasting, particularly when a company is ready to offer good products at a low price.

According to Cherian, the reason why Chinese phone makers have cut through this image problem and become successful in the retail segment is because they have successfully converted the classy brand game in smartphones into a more rowdy and democratic commodity play. Though the brands do advertise, they are all labelled in the consumer's mind as 'Chinese phones'. Penetration has been easy once the game was changed.

'The most important reason why Chinese image hasn't affected smartphones under multiple brands is that they are cheap. Over the years the cheap mobile phones have become better looking and desirable for most Indian aspirants. In fact, for them, their manufacturing origin has become an advantage,' he said.

Border row: How mature governments turned it into a take-off point instead of a setback

A question often asked is whether the seventy-three-day border clash between Indian and Chinese troops in 2017 has damaged bilateral relations to the extent that it affected mutual trade and investments.

Every effort should be made by the two countries to settle the boundary dispute, which has been a festering wound in the relationship since the 1962 war and has done no good to either country. Border disputes and mutual suspicion only help the arms industry while they distract governments from their task of economic development and maintaining law and order. They also take away crucial opportunities for collaboration and interexchange of ideas and development efforts.

Which is why the re-emergence of serious dispute in 2017 at the Doklam site is viewed with serious concern. It goes to the credit of both the Modi- and Xi-led governments that they did not allow this dispute to cause serious fissures in the relationship.

There is really no sign of a setback owing to the border row, leading many to believe that the issue of political risk for businesspeople is overstated. Many concluded that trade and business will go ahead based on economic realities and profit valuations instead of political differences that date back to 1962 when both India and China were stuck in an economic morass.

Data released by the China's General Administration of Customs shows that bilateral trade rose to an all-time high of USD 84.44 billion in 2017, which saw the row at Doklam emerging in June and ending in August. Note that bilateral trade stagnated at around USD 70 billion in the previous years. India's exports to China rose by 40 per cent from 2016 levels to reach USD 16.34 billion. The USD 100 billion target set by leaders of the two sides in 2015 has now been reached by the end of 2018. (Chinese data are for the calendar year.)

Foreign direct investments from China also saw a marked increase of nearly USD 9 billion in less than two years after 2017. Between 2000 and 2017, a measly USD 1.78 billion flowed in, according to figures released by the Department for Promotion of Industry and Internal Trade at India's Ministry of Commerce & Industry.

The Indian government says that investment flows from China between 2014 and 2019, the first term of the Modi government, exceeded USD 4 billion. But the Indian government is looking at the small numbers relating to inflows from Mainland China without taking into account massive inflows from subsidiaries of Chinese companies in Singapore, the US and elsewhere. An estimated USD 9–10 billion has flowed in so far.

'The Doklam dispute has added to India's prestige in the eyes of Chinese who were a little surprised that Indian troops would stand up to Chinese forces for so long. It also showed that Chinese authorities were not interested in continuing the clashes, and wanted an amicable settlement,' an Indian business consultant said, requesting anonymity. 'Chinese investors carefully study signals from their government, and they have concluded that Beijing really wants friendship with India.'

In my interviews with Chinese businesspeople, the question of political risks flowing from the border dispute regularly comes up because it remains a factor of reckoning. The only issue is how important it is to a particular business. For instance, Chinese mobile companies like Xiaomi and Internet business giants like Alibaba and Tencent have gone into the Indian market with considerable energy while state-owned companies (SEOs) from China have been reluctant.

'For private companies from China, political risk is a 10 per cent factor in making investment decisions about India. For state-owned companies, it could be 80 per cent,' said Li Jian, who runs Chinese consultancy company Draphant in India.

Indeed, the giant SOEs from China in energy, banking, telecommunications and a variety of other sectors have mostly stayed away from India. The only exceptions are where SOEs use India to provide some basic services as they do in any other country of the world. They include Air China and China Eastern Airlines and Industrial and Commercial Bank of China (ICBC) running a branch in Mumbai. Of course, part of the reason is the government reluctance to extend necessary licences to foreign businesses in strategic areas.

Another consultant, Melody Meng, who runs CASME Development Management Co. Ltd, said she had received different feedback from her Chinese clients altogether.

'Border disputes tend to take the relationship between China and India up and down from time to time. Chinese investors consider this very seriously, and some would put the risk factor at 60 per cent,' she said.

A third Chinese company advised me to look at the situation differently. Chinese investors will go where there is profit to be made. They have taken a lot more risks going into politically unstable places like certain African countries, Myanmar and Venezuela because they saw good business prospects.

Some would say there is the role of government in deciding the direction of Chinese investments, including those from private companies, in strategic sectors like telecommunications and Internet databases businesses, in foreign countries. This explains the special interests shown by Chinese companies in a wide range of mobile phone and applications companies which include e-commerce and payment systems.

India has a different kind of foreign policy risk. It must perform a balancing act at the international level. It is a member of the Regional Comprehensive Economic Partnership (RCEP), which aims to bring about a free trade agreement—reduction or removal of tariff for trade between its members.[3] The club's members include members of the Association of Southeast Asian Nations (Brunei, Cambodia, Indonesia, Laos, Malaysia, Myanmar, the Philippines, Singapore, Thailand and Vietnam) and the six Indo-Pacific states of China, Japan, South Korea, India, Australia and New Zealand. India has to play along, but it knows fully well that imposing high trade tax barriers against Chinese imports is one of the best ways to protect the local industry and guide it towards growth. China, which has for decades protected its industry against foreign business aggression, is now demanding an end to trade barriers on the ground of globalization. It's a difficult tightrope walk for New Delhi. It needs to hang on until India achieves greater economic strength and adds at least another USD 1 trillion to the USD 2.7 trillion economy or, as Prime Minister Narendra Modi predicted, becomes a USD 5 trillion economy by 2024.

It must be realized that both Modi and Xi Jinping are into their second terms and thinking in terms of the legacy they would leave behind. Resolving the border row would ensure them a place in history. This is hugely tempting for leaders who have reached the pinnacle of all that can be achieved within their countries. The big challenge for them is to avoid major sacrifices, which will happen during any boundary settlement, and major political resistance at home.

9

MOVING TOWARDS A USD 5 TRILLION ECONOMY: POLICY LEARNINGS FROM CHINA

I was once asked by a top official in the government in New Delhi to name one policy in China that can be implemented without much trouble.

The reply was an easy one. Identify a bunch of officers in three different fields, give them specific goals to achieve in a fixed timeline of two weeks or so. The tasks may be small but the officials will be given no opportunity to explain why it could not be done.

'This is possible in the communist system. My officer here would have excuses ready even as I am giving him a task,' the official said.

Many of us can go on and on discussing the problems without political and administrative systems but avoid taking the bull by the horns. But there are some politicians and officials in New Delhi and across the country who deliver significant results within the same system.

There is enough reason to be open-minded and learn from China. The country's achievements in a range of areas—economic growth, poverty alleviation, raising the standards of living of over a billion people, self-reliant advancement in science and technology, and eye-catching progress in culture, arts and sports—are unrivalled by any other country in a comparable time-frame.

This section presents the views of three scholars, including two Indians, who have been closely studying China for several years.

How different is Chinese governance?

Manoranjan Mohanty, a China scholar, author and Distinguished Professor at the Council for Social Development in New Delhi, explains the policy situation eloquently in one sentence: 'Policymaking in China has three steps while in India one-and-a-half steps.'

Explaining the stages of policymaking, he says that in China the top leadership puts out an idea with a broad direction as the first step. Then there are discussions by academic institutions, central and provincial governmental bodies, NGOs and some cases of actual experience on that subject are also reported and discussed in public. In this second stage both Party and state agencies ask their institutes' academics and researchers to collect evidence from relevant fields and submit it to them. Based on this, the third step is taken and a draft resolution is moved in the Communist Party's Central Committee, if it is important, or in the State Council, the relevant ministry or in the Standing Committee of the National People's Congress (NPC), which is the parliament. Sometimes there is another intermediate step before the final decision. A draft decision is put out for public discussion, even public hearings and for obtaining views of the wider public, including international opinion. Scholarly inputs, wide range of public discussions are thus ensured before a policy is made in China.

There is very little debate in the NPC, which is regarded as a rubber stamp parliament. Chinese rulers have a lot more faith in the abilities of subject experts, business representatives and Communist officials with hands-on administrative experience than in the parliament. China also has a political advisory body, Chinese People's Political Consultative Conference (CPPCC) which has representatives from professional and industry bodies, Party backed religious associations and state-owned companies.

'In India, unfortunately, a favoured group of advisers puts up a proposal and the Prime Minister's Office decides. There is half a step taken in the Parliament for minor amendments sometimes,' Mohanty said. Important policies are passed with a voice vote and without discussion in Parliament. Of course, some campaigns and strongly debated legislation succeed from time to time, though not satisfactorily.

The irony is that India's democratic system is not utilized to its normal capacity in decision-making. It is evident, particularly in economic decisions. In China too there are favoured advisers of the top leadership. Some decisions are taken by that group and the wider discussion is used to legitimize that.

China is of course more effective in the implementation process compared to India, Mohanty said.

In private discussions, Indian businessmen draw comparison between Indian and Chinese courts, which generally supports business projects as long as they are approved by the government. The Right to Information Act (RTI) and Public Interest Litigation (PIL) which often block or delay projects on issues like pollution are not in vogue in China, they point out. There is an element of contradiction in such complaints because it is the very same Indian businessmen who rush to courts to fight battles when they perceive injustice to themselves.

Both countries have to learn from one another and others and choose their own paths.

An important question is: Did China bargain better to get advantages out of foreign investors before giving away market access?

According to Mohanty, China bargained using market access as a lever to open up and allow FDI. India may not have played the bargaining chip as effectively.

There is a debate in India about the logic behind allowing 100 per cent FDI to foreign investors and whether this will deny local industry the opportunity to learn and grow.

'The Open Door policy and the reforms in China produced high economic growth, better livelihood, world class urbanization, global status and national pride, but with serious problems of inequality, regional disparities, corruption, environmental degradation, social alienation and many other things. In my view all layers of production and distribution, from villages and towns to the national, continental and global level, even in a high-tech era, have to be mutually dependent on equitable terms. Therefore the terms of global capital flow have to be subjected to that logic,' he said. The thesis in Mohanty's book *China's Transformation: The Success Story and the Success Trap* addresses this issue.

I asked if he thought that adapting its Belt and Road Initiative would result in China's overwhelming influence on the politically linked project development system.

'In BRI China's influence will necessarily dominate. This is why the way it was initiated was faulty. It should have followed the AIIB (Asian Infrastructure Investment Bank) path of consulting with participating countries. But Xi Jinping is determined to go ahead with this as a Chinese drive on a global platform, so all countries and organizations have to cope with this and utilize the opportunities. There are bound to be countervailing movements whenever hegemonic activities appear on the scene,' Mohanty said.

In BRI's foreign projects, Indian developers won't succeed against Chinese contractors in open bidding if they wish to take advantage of the Belt program—what do you say?

'No, Indian investors, contractors and experts can operate as autonomous entities in all those countries and can compete well. There are no formal ban flowing from Indian government›s opposition to BRI,'

Scholar who has worked with the Prime Minister's Office

Listening to Sudheendra Kulkarni, well-known author and adviser to former prime minister Atal Behari Vajpayee, was a worthwhile experience.

He identified three lessons from China for speedy economic growth in India:

- Modernization of infrastructure
- Development of self-reliant strengths in high-technology industries; and

- Development of human capital by giving high priority to good-quality education both at school and university levels.

India began the journey of reforms fifteen years after China. India and China were more or less at the same level of economic development in the 1970s before New Delhi seemed to lose its way.

China also has the advantage of strong linkages between the state and provincial governments, something that is difficult in the Indian system where each politician is bent on building his own image and career.

We may have learnt some team spirit in cricket but in governance, this is still a far cry.

Kulkarni cites the example of China's successful railway growth to explain its determination in building infrastructure. Independent India inherited 53,396 km of railway network in 1947 while China only had 27,000 km of railway at that time. 'Cut to 2019 when we see India has a railway route length of 67,312 km, and growing at a meagre average rate of about 400 km per year. In contrast, China's railway network has a total length of 131,000 km, of which 29,000 km are high-speed railways. There are no high-speed trains in India.

'It's evident that India needs to modernize its infrastructure at an accelerated speed,' he said.

The second factor to be noted is China's determination to be a science and technology centre as a means to be an economic superpower. The link between science and technological excellence and economic growth is still tenuous and scientists are not rewarded for their innovation and discoveries.

China encouraged its industries, providing them not just financing but scientific support from its universities and laboratories to grow to an extent where it came to be called the 'factory to the world'.

'The moral of the story: India cannot follow the path of dependence on other countries when it comes to hi-tech. It must build its own self-reliant strengths. The Indian market is big enough to warrant this approach since India's population is now close to that of China, and also since its development needs are enormous,' said Kulkarni.

Starting in the 1990s, China initiated two projects to push forward development of science, technology and culture with the goal of enhancing the country's international competitiveness and training high-level manpower to meet the demands of industry arising out of the economic reforms in 1978. One of them called Project 211 had 112 institutions, while the more advanced club of thirty-nine universities was called Project 985. These arrangements were besides the top echelons of nine universities, or C9.

'Enrich human capital by giving high priority to providing good-quality education both at school and university levels. We need to observe how China is promoting its top universities to become world leaders in research and innovation and helping them commercialize their R&D. This is evident [in] this single example. Tsinghua Unigroup Ltd, a company controlled by Tsinghua University, plans to invest 300 billion yuan (USD 47 billion) in a bid to become the world's third-biggest chipmaker—behind Intel and Samsung. This is a strategic priority for China to become self-reliant in a sensitive industry. The annual revenue of Zhejiang University is 10.9 billion yuan and of Peking University is 8.6 billion yuan,' he said.

Kulkarni pointed out that three important features have enabled top Chinese universities to become world-class. One, not just the C9 League universities but also the thirty-nine leading universities under Project 985 enjoy a very high degree of empowerment. The presidents of these universities have vice-ministerial ranks in the central government. (In contrast, the vice chancellors of Indian universities have a rank below that of the secretary of the education department in state governments.)

Two, China's government agencies, research institutions and even schools all look to other countries' experiences for inspiration to improve their own functioning. Their reform plans always have a component of international comparative study to benchmark against developed countries and draw upon best practices. Chinese universities, like the ones in US, UK and Canada (and unlike in India), consciously enrol a large number of foreign students and hire foreign faculty. Very soon, China will have more foreign students than the US universities. Chinese government pursues a long-term plan, with the requisite political will and financial support to help Chinese universities become the best in the world.

Three, good-quality education is the greatest force of social transformation and nation-building. This is true about every country. China has understood this very well. Eradication of illiteracy was a major campaign launched in the Mao era itself. In the past four decades, China has simultaneously focused on improving both school education and university education.

'India should especially look at China's stunning success in improving its university education to world-class levels,' Kulkarni said.

China launched an ambitious initiative called Project 211 in 1995 to raise the research and academic standards of National Key Universities. The name of the project derives from an abbreviation of the twenty-first century and 100 (approximate number of participating universities). China today has 116 institutions of higher education (about 6 per cent of the total) designated as 211 Project institutions for having met high scientific, technical, and human resources standards. These train four-fifths of doctoral students, two-thirds of graduate students, half of students from abroad and one-third of undergraduates, and consume 70 per cent of scientific research funding.

China spends USD 250 billion or 4 per cent of GDP on education. In terms of producing graduates, China has overtaken the United States and the combined university systems of European Union countries. Chinese students are also doing better than their American counterparts in mathematics, sciences, computing and engineering, the subjects most relevant to innovation and technological advance. In 2013, 40 per cent of Chinese graduates completed their studies in a STEM (science, technology, engineering and math) subject—more than twice the share of US graduates, he said.

Why China's model cannot be replicated in India

The problem of low development is that you have less money and knowledge which are necessary to build infrastructure. China offered attractive terms to obtain foreign investments during the first phase of its development process. It has some political advantages. The government is the only landlord, making it easy to allocate land for projects of all kinds.

'In some ways, China's ecosystem makes it easier to build infrastructure and to attract foreign capital,' Julian Evans-Pritchard, China economist for consulting firm, Capital Economist, told me in an interview. 'The way labour laws are structured and the government's tax incentives have made China an attractive investment destination,' he said.

In the early years of economic reforms, Beijing gave tax exemptions to foreign players and charged taxes on local industry. Such a move would be impossible in a democracy like India.

'What China is able to do is quite hard to replicate in other countries, because you can't just take away people's land, you cannot give foreign investors special treatment over and above local firms. But this is how China managed to build up a strong manufacturing base,' Evans-Pritchard said.

The Chinese model involved pandering to the demands and whims of foreign investors to have them on board, and later put foreign companies under terrible pressure once the domestic industry grew and the country's bargaining capability enhanced. Beijing has been widely accused of forcing China-based foreign companies to surrender their technologies to local players. Accusers include the associations of American and European businesses besides government officials in Washington. Can India enrich itself with this method?

Firstly, there are very few joint ventures between Indian and foreign companies. Even the newcomers from China have shown a marked preference for going alone instead of tying up with an Indian partner. Secondly, forced technology transfers can result in litigation and Indian courts are unlikely to deny justice to a foreign company for the sake of protecting the local ones. In China, several local companies work in tandem, each complementing the other in implementing a new idea whether stolen from a foreign source or otherwise. Such an ecosystem does not exist in India.

What India can learn from China's politically backed AI growth

Chinese President Xi Jinping has tried to exhort businesses and scientific research teams engaged in artificial intelligence and robotics on different occasions. He asked Communist leaders to 'ensure that our country marches in the front ranks where it comes to theoretical research in this important area of AI [artificial intelligence], and occupies the high ground in critical and AI core technologies.' He also asked them to 'ensure that critical and core AI technologies are firmly grasped in our own hands.'

Analysts said China's political system and the government's eagerness to support technological advancement were key reasons why it could build infrastructure such as cloud computing and software engineering workforce and become a big player in AI.

Two of the world's top fifteen AI giants, including the drone maker DJI, are Chinese. The other is chipset maker HiSilicon. Three of the world's top three robotics companies—Shenzhen YueJiang Technology Co. Ltd, Rokid Corporation Ltd. and Um, Define Robot—are based in China, while the fourth is a Sino-American venture called ZongMu Technology.

Given the fact that software and Internet companies are mostly behind the growth of AI, it is important to look at how these firms are doing in different countries.

Of the top thirty companies ranked in terms of Internet market capitalization by the 2019 Mary Marker report—a widely accepted yardstick—seven are Chinese and eighteen others are based in the US. None of them are Indian. This is significant because the higher echelons of many of the American IT and Internet companies, including Google CEO Sundar Pichai and Microsoft chief executive Satya Nadella, happen to be people of Indian origin.

In an article, state-run *Global Times* said, 'It is fair to say that India's tech prowess, still largely confined to IT services, is nowhere close to China, one of the twin engines in the tech world that now derives most of its power from Internet-driven innovation.'

The paper went on to ask, 'How could India, which embarked on IT services development in the 1960s, become invisible in the Internet world nowadays?' The article concluded that India was losing its best talent to Silicon Valley and this was hampering the growth of its Internet-related business. 'In the case of India, a continuation of obsession with Silicon Valley would only distance itself from global tech leadership.'

One may not accept the somewhat sweeping diagnosis in the article, but the Indian IT sector, which is closely related to the growth of AI, needs to do a lot of soul-searching about how it fell behind the race, while China with its controls on academic freedom managed to produce exceptional companies and talent in a few short decades.

To most independent analysts, China is set to take the lead in the field of AI as Chinese companies try to put its awesome power to revamp not just the production process across the vast nation, including its rust belt comprising old-time plants producing steel, metal parts and electricity.

AI is also helping in the establishment of a system of constant innovation in product design in line with market needs and matching production with delivery schedules. AI backed robots are replacing workers by the thousands without causing much of an uproar partly because the government is channelizing the surplus labour in other industries and partly because the news media is not in the habit of picking up stories of dissent.

It is important for Indian business to watch China's progress in AI and robotics because a number of Indian start-ups in Bangalore, Hyderabad and elsewhere have begun to make presentations in their attempts to get outsourcing jobs from Chinese technology companies.

There may be a bit of hurdle concerning trust in this area. Though China is generally open to attracting new technologies from abroad, Chinese companies are extremely reluctant when it comes to situations where they are vulnerable to losing control of technologies that they already possess or have developed.

Besides, technology involves a race and being left behind is not going to help India's development which includes its exports and influence in the world.

The Indian government must realize that AI capabilities can help create new possibilities and business models like self-driving cars that can disrupt the transportation industry. Use of robots in factory floors can overhaul product quality and make Indian goods more desirable in the export market.

It may be politically important for the ruling party to chase the goal of higher employment and shun labour-reducing technologies like robotics but in the end Indian companies and exports don't grow and the country remains caught in the low-growth cycle. Technology, if deployed in essential areas, can help break through the logjam of low growth.

India's IT companies know that AI presents an opportunity to go beyond their capabilities in enterprise solutions and extend their ability to serve a wider range of functions and industries.

In the coming years, a crucial deciding factor of world influence would be which country builds a larger AI talent pool and a broader AI R&D infrastructure to make sustained progress. This is where the government and training institutions have an important role to play.

Being a Communist country helps companies in China when it comes to deploying new technologies like facial recognition which is often difficult in democratic countries like the US, said William A. Carter, deputy director and fellow, Technology Policy Program at the Center for Strategic and International Studies.

'China does have strengths in terms of application development and deployment, and has the potential to take the lead in the deployment of some technologies like autonomous vehicles and facial recognition where ethical, social and policy hurdles may impede deployment in the US and other parts of the world,' Carter said.

Beijing is going all guns to acquire superiority in this crucial field. Gregory Allen with the Center for a New American Security was recently quoted as saying that the US Defense Advanced Research Projects Agency is spending the most on research and development, at USD 2 billion over five years. On the other hand, the province of Shanghai, which has a city government, is planning to spend USD 15 billion over ten years.

'So literally we have the US federal government at present at risk of being outspent by a provincial government of China,' Allen said.

AI is everywhere in China today as the government encourages different segments of society to work on it. Hospitals are constantly hitting headlines for conducting complex surgeries using AI-driven robots. The official news agency Xinhua demonstrated a robot that can write up reports after sorting through a mass of news material.

The best praise comes from your ability to tense up nerves in the homes of your rivals, and this is what appears to have happened in the US if we go by the sharp reactions emanating from the Trump administration.

'Continued American leadership in Artificial Intelligence is of paramount importance to maintaining the economic and national security of the United States,' US President Donald Trump was quoted as saying in an official press release accompanying the order which exhorted American companies to do more in the field.

Washington has tried to shut off the flow of technology from the US to China, made it difficult for China's main technology company Huawei Technologies and fined another telecom firm, ZTE. Some analysts say that Chinese corporate and defence-related research in areas like AI and 5G technologies can hold and thrive on their own even if information flow from the Western world is shut off. China is already leading in several segments of businesses like autonomous vehicles, facial recognition and certain kinds of drones.

The US-based Allen Institute of Artificial Intelligence caused a flurry recently by asserting that China is a close second after the United States when it comes to producing the top 10 per cent most-cited research papers in artificial intelligence. The US contribution is 29 per cent and China accounts 26 per cent of such papers.

'The US still is ahead in AI development capabilities but the gap between the US and China is closing rapidly because of the significant new AI investments in China,' said Bart Selman, president-elect of the Association for the Advancement of AI, a professional organization.

But it has its own share of challenges. China is far behind the US in production of semiconductors, ahead in the number of potential users and has about half the number of AI experts and roughly half the number of AI companies. Though China may be marching ahead very fast at the moment, its long-term potential is about half that of the US, experts say.

Beijing is striving for that crucial turning point when it will acquire greater strength in the field of semiconductors and is ready to invest heavily for this purpose. Washington may have to use some amount of political and diplomatic muscle to ensure Japan and South Korea do not eagerly share their technological resources in such crucial areas.

China's capabilities in image and face recognition are possibly the best in the world, partly because government controls have made it easier to generate data from a wide range of sources like banks, mobile phone companies and the social media.

'These capabilities arise out of the use of deep learning on very large data sets. In general, China has the advantage of having more real-world data to train AI systems than any other country,' Selman said.

Some of the other areas where China has shown significant advances are natural language processing (in Chinese only) and UAV swarming.

'China also has unique capabilities that are not found in the US or Europe. I'm thinking of electronic payment platforms (e.g. AliPay) and the super-app WeChat that provide an advanced platform for the rapid introduction of further AI technologies,' Selman said.

What has India to offer Chinese investors

A major challenge is competing with several countries trying to attract foreign investments, particularly of the Chinese variety. Countries like Vietnam are better placed because they offer a Chinese food and cultural environment and have tax treaties with China, which India does not.

What India has is the advantage of a massive market which is already enticing hundreds of Chinese companies. Attracting this kind of investment will push Indian companies to do better because the Chinese are masters in price reduction to capture market size. But an excess of such push and pull factor will persuade a lot of Indian company managements to sell off their assets to Chinese players at high price and move aside. The government must strike a balance, and this is a difficult task. China used foreign investments to bring about massive growth by opening up its market bit by bit.

Why should China encourage Indian IT companies and even push Chinese companies to invest in India? There are quite a few reasons, which many Chinese companies are unaware of.

Awareness of one another is a major problem between India and China, but China is at an advantage because its business success is more in international focus with as many admirers as critics. It is a question of whether we have done enough to build awareness about India among the Chinese.

Chinese presence in India has been most prominent in the western states of Gujarat and Maharashtra although there is a growing interest in the National Capital Region and the southern states. The presence of Chinese investors covers the Ahmedabad–Vadodara cluster for light engineering and electrical equipment sector and in the Mumbai–Pune cluster, they have shown interest in heavy equipment and plastic components. Chinese investments in the Delhi NCR cluster are in segments like electronics, electrical machinery, auto components, real estate. In the Bengaluru cluster, money has flowed into IT and the real estate business. Andhra Pradesh has seen Chinese investments coming in light engineering and solar modules.

By 2025, India consumer market is expected to touch USD 3.6 trillion, according to a Boston Consulting Group study. The government has pledged to nearly double the size of the economy to USD 5 trillion by 2024.

India is the world's fastest-growing economy and figures among the top ten countries as a destination in terms of freedom of information. Some think tanks, including the Wharton school and Ernst & Young, regard it as one of the world's most attractive investment destinations. Some consultants have said India is a top choice for technology-related multinational companies for establishing research and development centres outside their home country. This is already evident in R&D investments made in India by Microsoft and other companies.

India does not have the kind of reputation that China has in the field of manufacturing but it has been ranked the sixth-largest manufacturing nation by UNIDO.

At 462 million, India has the second largest number of Internet users, after China. It has an urban population of 377 million, which ensures a good market for consumer goods. Several Chinese companies, including white goods maker Haier, are already getting a taste of the buying power of urban Indian middle class.

To Chinese investors looking at India, the government has promised as follows:

- Ready land in clusters and single-window clearance
- Very attractive financial incentives
- Huge talent pool and support for skilled manpower
- Support for innovation and R&D
- The world's fastest-growing market

But there are serious complaints about land allotment and projects are stuck because the governments in the states are unable to deliver the necessary land plots after acquisition because of local protests and court litigations.

India has favourable demographics; the average national age expected to be twenty-nine years in 2020 should be a major draw for foreign investors. A young nation offers a massive talent pool and a huge consumer market.

The government has taken a series of development measures, opening up investment opportunities for foreigners, including the Chinese. They include:

Digital India: Ensuring that government services are made available to citizens electronically by improving online infrastructure and by increasing internet connectivity. Empowering the country digitally involves development and enhancement of:

- broadband highways
- public internet access programme
- information for everyone
- early harvest programmes
- universal access to phones
- IT for jobs skill development

- eKranti (electronic delivery of services)
- electronic manufacturing (target net zero import)

Smart cities: Urban renewal and retrofitting programme with a mission to develop 100 cities all over the country, making them citizen friendly and sustainable. It allows 100 per cent foreign direct investments with no need for an Indian partner. It also encourages public–private partnership. The highlights of the programme are:

- opportunity of over USD 150 billion
- 107 Smart Cities by 2022
- 90 cities already shortlisted for design and construction
- USD 15 billion budgetary support over the next four years for sewerage systems and waste management
- 500 cities under rejuvenation (AMRUT)
- 20 million houses under 'Housing for All' by 2022
- Start-up India, aimed at promoting bank financing for start-up ventures to boost entrepreneurship and encourage start-ups with jobs creation
- Skill India includes National Skill Development Mission, National Policy for Skill Development and Entrepreneurship 2015, Pradhan Mantri Kaushal Vikas Yojana (PMKVY) scheme and the Skill Loan scheme.

Make in India: Initiative to encourage multinational as well as domestic companies to manufacture their products in India. Launched in September 2014, the goal is to make India the most preferred global manufacturing destination

Electronics sector is one of the twenty-five focus sectors.

GST: Single biggest reform. It includes:

- Reduction in multiplicity of taxes
- Mitigation of cascading/double taxation
- Efficient neutralization of taxes, especially for exports

- Development of a common national market
- Simpler tax regime, fewer rates and exemptions

Industrial corridors:

Delhi Mumbai Industrial Corridor (DMIC)

- USD 100 billion opportunity
- Reduce transportation time of goods from fourteen days to fourteen hours
- 1504 km of Dedicated Freight Corridor (DFC) intersects seven states—Delhi, UP, Haryana, Rajasthan, MP, Gujarat and Maharashtra
- Twenty-four investment regions/industrial areas
- Eight sustainable industrial cities with world-class infrastructure

Second-largest start-up ecosystem:

Start-ups: There are more than 200,000 start-ups in India at a total valuation exceeding USD 50 billion. There are 200-plus incubators and accelerators that have released funding worth USD 9.5 billion since January 2016.

Initiatives taken under the government's National Skill Development Corporation programme includes training of 3.3 million students across thirty-three sectors in a year.

Currently:

- India has the second-largest number of engineers and scientists
- It is the second-largest English-speaking population in the world
- It has educational institutes of global repute like Indian Institute of Technology and Indian Institute of Management across several campuses

- The working age population is expected to increase to 64 per cent by 2021
- The average age is predicted to be twenty-nine years in 2020, lower than that in China and the US
- It is expected to be home to 25 per cent of the world's skilled workforce by 2025
- About 1.5 million graduates pass out in India every year
- 250 million people expected to join the Indian workforce by 2030
- Electronics Development Fund: Fund of funds model—22 daughter funds, with cumulative corpus of USD 1 billion

National Centres of Excellence:

- Large Area Flexible Electronics (NCFLEX) at IIT-Kanpur
- Technology on Internal Security (NCETIS) at IIT-Bombay
- Internet of Things (IoT) in Bengaluru, Gurugram, Visakhapatnam and Ahmedabad
- Electropreneur Park at University of Delhi
- Incubation centers at IIT Patna (medical electronics)
- IIITM Kochi (consumer electronics)
- TIDE- Scheme for Technology Incubation and Development of Entrepreneurs in area of Electronics, ICT & Management
- iCAS for Set Top Boxes (STBs):The Indian Conditional Access System is successfully developed

10

PEOPLE-TO-PEOPLE LINKAGES

A Chinese businessman's impressions of India

What follows is a fictionalized account of some interesting things I have learnt in my interviews about Chinese business attitudes towards India.

Lin Lin's seven-year-old wifely instinct sensed an oddity in her husband's demeanour as he stepped into their American-style living room after spending a few days in India. Her husband is usually upbeat or downbeat about business prospects after a foreign visit, sometimes raging over the ineptness of his executives or the restraints that came down on him from 'high up'. On occasions when he returned from Europe via Bangkok, she detected secret happiness in him. Or, perhaps she imagined it.

Looking at him now, Lin Lin wondered how much he had changed since that distant day when she saw him denouncing Western imperialism at a Communist Party meeting in college. She had begun to worship her future *loagong* (literally 'get old together') or husband, almost instantly, and this did not change for years even after he adopted an English name, Peter, and rose to become the vice president of the international division in his manufacturing company.

Things had begun to change rapidly in recent years after he decided to buy a house in the US and send their daughter to an American boarding school. Lin Lin would sometimes go on solo trips to meet the daughter and her financial advisor, a US-based Chinese expat who helped them manage secret bank accounts and investments.

The couple were merely following a trend, a wave sweeping through thousands of Chinese who felt the need to protect their funds after rising to the high point of wealth or reaching somewhere in the midpoint with a few million dollars to spare.

Economists estimate that about USD 1 trillion of the country's savings has been siphoned off to foreign destinations by business executives and corrupt officials helping the Chinese to emerge as the biggest buyer of properties in Australia, New Zealand, Singapore, Africa, and parts of the United States and Europe.

(No Chinese investor considered investing in the Indian property market, which offers many times more return than most other places that they have gone to. The indifference towards India's real estate market is caused by legal hurdles on foreign property ownership and uncertainties about the Indian market.)

He was now a different person in as much as the Communist Party has become unrecognizable to old dedicated members who still hung pictures and posters of Mao Zedong and other early Communist leaders on their walls. The Party, which began 'feeling the pebbles while crossing the stream' by introducing economic reforms in 1979, was now posing as the most aggressive champion of globalization while the US was retracing its steps like a frightened warrior shielding itself. What irony!

Lin Lin's husband had just returned from his second visit to India, which launched economic reforms a dozen years after China, and has since been unsure about handling English-speaking Western investors, leave aside the Chinese. He looked plain confused this time. She decided to preserve the probing until breakfast the next morning, but he was already complaining.

'Everyone speaks English in India. But, it's difficult to understand them until you become accustomed to their accent,' he started while pouring some wine at the dinner table.

Peter had visited someplace in India where liquor is out of bounds. 'The first day, no liquor. Terrible. We needed a government licence or something to buy liquor. Fortunately, our fixers got a week's permit the second day,' he moaned.

The hosts had invited his team for dinner the first evening, but it started two hours after his usual dinnertime of 6 p.m. The consulting company had warned him about the odd timing, about the wine and food restrictions. But one can never be prepared to suffer denial of regular food like beef and pork, and only water or coke to wash down oil-laced vegetables. He looked at the notepad on his phone to describe a yellow bean porridge called *dal*, which tasted like Chinese medicine, and fried balls called, well, *pakoda*. Of course, he had praised every dish wholesomely while his stomach turned and he craved for the boxes of noodles in his suitcase.

'KTV, women,' she asked coyly wondering what her husband and his colleagues did after business meetings are over.

'These people have no idea of fun, no drinking, no karaoke. And their jokes . . . too many jokes . . . they make no sense in translation,' he cribbed. 'How can you do business without a good dinner and some fun?' Peter asked, glancing at the gilded statue of Caishen, the Chinese god of wealth, in one corner of the living room.

Lin Lin had quietly placed a small bronze idol of Ganesha, hoping both gods would bring luck to the family and protect their daughter. But Peter need not know about it.

Peter rambled on about the endless vistas of opportunities that India can offer to his company, which was battling the twin challenges of machine overcapacity and low sales. Vietnam was already crowded with Chinese competitors and India offered a good alternative market. He broke into a rare ironic smile, and mumbled that Indians would ask for big discounts if they knew how desperate his company was for sales.

But penetration seemed difficult. Most Indian buyers thought in small numbers, offering to buy less now and slowing increase their purchases over time. Among the clients he met, some didn't have enough budget and some lacked commercial guts.

'The Indians talk of such small deals. And, they negotiate the price endlessly. But we will still go ahead and do something,' he said.

Lin Lin was hoping to join him to a visit to India. 'Will you go there again?'

'Yes. The company wants me to go again and again, do anything to clear the inventories,' he said while yawning into silence.

Natural linkages and official handshakes

The India brand lives and thrives in almost every Chinese city and town in the form of yoga training schools, Bollywood movies watched in theatres and over the Internet, and even in traditional Chinese restaurants that usually have a 'curry' dish with Indian spices like turmeric on the menu. Thousands of Indian and Chinese students get in touch with each other as they study in US and Australian universities.

Not just Bollywood but also Indian television dramas, particularly those concerning mythologies like the Mahabharata and the Ramayana, have become hugely popular among the Internet-surfing Chinese population. There is a following for Indian gods not in the sense of worship, which does not come naturally to the Chinese nearly seventy-five years after the Communist-controlled government virtually banned religion. Indian gods are adored more in the sense of them being heroes and fascinating characters in the way that Chinese love or 'worship' great warriors and scholars of the past.

'Nowadays, there are many Indian movies and TV series watched in China. Many people in China are followers of Krishna. They love Lord Vishnu and Shiva. They want to know the stories regarding these deities,' said Jiang Jingkui, director at the Center of South Asian Studies at Peking University in Beijing.

Dozens of cleverly prepared and nuanced documents have been signed by governments of the two countries, calling for people to people exchanges over the past decades.

The ritual of agreement signing has been going on since 1954 when the then prime minister Jawaharlal Nehru and China's first premier Zhou Enlai signed the Panchsheel, with each side promising to abide by the five principles of mutual respect, non-aggression, non-interference, equality, and cooperation and peaceful coexistence. Leaders from the two countries continue to mention the Panchsheel during formal meetings although they know that the five principles remain, to a large extent, as principles waiting to be implemented.

Officials from India occasionally remind their Chinese counterparts that India was the first country outside the socialist bloc nations like Russia to establish diplomatic relations with the People's Republic of China in 1950. Much of this official talk is presented in the news media of the two countries but most people believe that ceremonial proclamations are just that. They don't link hearts, which requires a different kind of endeavour.

Leaders from both sides speak about developing a people-to-people relationship for tourism but such talk goes unheard in the government departments. During the past years the Chinese emerged as the world's biggest travellers and dozens of countries scrambled to attract a large slice of this business; India's ministries of tourism and aviation pretended as if they knew nothing of it. The India Tourism office did not have an Indian official for three years, until recently. Air India flies a single route from Shanghai and all other Indian airlines see no opportunity in China. Meanwhile, China's airline companies fly along more than a dozen routes from China to India.

Agreements will still be signed and speeches made. But it must be recognized that paper signing within the confines of government halls with carpeted floors and chandelier-filled ceilings do not reach the people.

Nothing compares with the overwhelming turnout of Indians during Chinese Premier Zhou Enlai's four visits to India during the heyday of '*Hindi Chini Bhai Bhai*', before the 1962 War, and the excited gathering of Chinese during Prime Minister Narendra Modi's recent visit to the historical city of Xian and Beijing. Nor does anything compare with the fan following for Rabindranath Tagore's poetry in China or the huge fan following for Bollywood movies, running in cinema halls across China at any given time in the past two years.

It must now be recognized that a people-to-people relationship is a meeting of hearts and any amount of documentation by term-serving officials will not make a difference. Here's another example of how public image works. Almost everyone in China has heard about India's proficiency in computer software. On the other hand, the China brand thrives in the remotest areas of India through Chinese consumer goods ranging from hairpins to smartphones.

This is a unique relationship that defies negative vibes from official machinery and the media. It is likely to grow with the expansion of cross-country tourism. Politicians and the media will have little opportunities but to respond positively to this unique friendship, and thus make business interactions more rewarding.

Communication challenges

If they send more Chinese to work for their companies in India, it works against them because this kind of image can fail them. Which is why most Chinese companies prefer to send just the main management professionals from headquarters while hiring locally for the rest.

In their chat platforms such as WeChat, Chinese managers post screenshots of messages from their Indian employees as a sign of their exasperation with dealing with the kind of personal challenges they have not faced back home. Messages posted on the chat groups read like these: 'I couldn't come today because I fell ill' or 'I couldn't come today because my child felt ill' or 'Mother sick.'

People fall ill in China as much as they do in India, but very few employees would cite this as reasons for skipping work. Almost no one questions the boss and dares to find excuses, even if the boss is a low-level manager.

Communication in India is also a challenge even when Chinese managers speak English because their language capabilities are not strong enough to accurately convey ideas and orders from the headquarters to the Indian staff.

Another challenge in India is the inadequate industrial ecosystem for foreign investors.

'Let me put this to our Indian friends: our shared understandings far outstrip our differences and our common interests far outweigh our frictions. China is willing and ready to inherit and take forward our traditional friendship and be a friend and partner of the Indian people. I hope the two sides will be free from mental inhibitions and meet each other halfway. Let us replace suspicion with trust, manage differences through dialogue, and build a future through cooperation,' said Wang Yi, Chinese foreign minister.

Indian ministers have voiced similar sentiment although they have not made much of an effort to connect with Chinese audiences. Visiting ministers from other countries who regularly appear on Chinese television make a lot more effort. If Indian officials do not get invited to television studios or for speaking arrangements in Chinese universities, it is an issue of inadequate and incorrect lobbying from our officials as well.

Indian diplomats must ask themselves if they have done enough to lobby in China and build on the massive cultural influence that India has had on the Chinese people for generations. The Indian embassy has arrangements to teach Indian music, dance and yoga at its premises in Beijing but it covers just a few dozen people.

China Radio International, the official radio network, has services in Hindi, Urdu, Bengali and Tamil. CRI sources experts and programmers for Urdu from Pakistan, for Bengali from Bangladesh and for Tamil from Sri Lanka. India could have put forward its claim and persuaded Chinese propaganda authorities to source at least one or two of the experts in the three languages from India. That would have ensured better coverage of India.

Chinese universities offering Urdu courses do not source their teachers from India. Even educated Chinese usually don't know that Urdu, Bengali and Tamil are spoken and read by millions in India.

In 2006, the ruling Communist Party's organ *People's Daily* elected Rabindranath Tagore as one of the fifty foreign personalities who have influenced modern Chinese thinking. This is a major political decision because the ruling party was sending out a signal to more than one billion Chinese about which foreigners to hold in high esteem. The government also ordered the creation of a twenty-eight-volume set on the complete works of Tagore, getting them translated into Chinese from the original Bengali.

Did we build on this opportunity to spread Tagore's message and enhance India's image in the Chinese mind? Our response was bureaucratic, which involved organizing a few workshops and conferences for experts to exchange views.

We need to connect with the common people in China in non-political areas to overcome the image erosion caused by border and other political differences. We must reach out through social media, organize courses in Hindi and other Indian languages, offer appreciation programmes for Indian movies and announce special programmes to attract Chinese tourists. Most important, such efforts must cover more than a dozen Chinese cities instead of just Beijing. A good way is to use linkages built by Indian restaurants and yoga schools across China.

Case study: A teacher's role in Chinese investments in India

It's important to see how well-prepared China is in dealing with India at all levels—business, cultural and political interactions.

There are a lot of reasons why Chinese companies are succeeding in India. Not many people in India would have heard of Prof. Jiang Jingkui, director at the Center of South Asian Studies at Peking University in Beijing. He has been teaching Hindi to Chinese students for nearly twenty-five years.

His students, many of whom are dealing with India, are now scattered in over fifty Chinese companies and institutions. They act as a communication bridge in offices of many Chinese companies, helping managers sent from China to deal with Indian customers and staff and make sense of a jumble of confused communication between the two sides. They also help negotiate problems in dealings with government agencies, cutting through misunderstanding and presenting the case of their employers in coherent Hindi.

Prof. Jiang, who has won some awards in India, earned high praise at a Hindi Day function in Beijing in 2018 from India's then external affairs minister, Sushma Swaraj. He is a well-known face for Indians in Beijing as he attends many events hosted by the Indian embassy. He was the first Chinese to earn a PhD in Hindi in 1996.

Currently, seventeen different universities and institutions offer degrees in Hindi. Besides, nine Chinese universities teach Urdu. Chinese universities also teach Bengali, Sanskrit and Pali, which is the language of many ancient Buddhist texts, an area of great interest for China.

The total number of Hindi graduates turned out by different Chinese universities may exceed 2000. This is apart from many others who are learning Hindi online just because they are excited about Bollywood and would like to listen to the dialogues in the original language.

Peking University, China's most respected educational institution, offers a four-year bachelor's degree in Hindi, followed by a master's degree. Each class at the bachelor's level has between fifteen and twenty-five students. The course is an interesting one, with students offered some kind of immersion programme on India, with studies about the history and culture and a taste of other Indian languages such as Sanskrit, Urdu, Bengali and Tamil, although the main focus is on learning Hindi.

'I think all my students have found jobs. There is a lot of demand among Chinese companies and institutions for people who know Hindi,' said Jiang, who has trained nearly 250 Hindi graduates.

Hindi qualified students also get jobs in Chinese government agencies and the media as well as in Hindi departments of various Chinese universities.

I asked how he saw the relationship between the Himalayan neighbours improving in the coming years.

'You have to realize that a vast number of Chinese are interested in knowing more about India. The perception is changing,' he said.

Speaking of political perception, Jiang said, 'Chinese people understand that even if India is not their friend, at least they are not our enemy. We respect each other. We do business with each other. For the common people in China, India is a good place.'

Jiang has visited India several times and feels that the common people in India think highly of China and want a good relationship between the two countries.

'I expect a lot of improvement in the relationship between the two countries. The amount of business between them is very low at present. This is going to improve a lot,' he said.

One area that needs attention is the expansion of the exchange programme between students in the two countries. The exchange programme for languages is currently minimal, covering just about fifty students a year.

This is an area where Indian and Chinese companies should step in. It costs little, but the goodwill generated would be lasting as students covered under the programme will play crucial roles in the relationship in the coming years.

Case study: Connecting musically: Indian ragas for Chinese ears

Listening to live recitals of maestros such as Amjad Ali Khan can be a rare treat if you live in China. Such shows have been taking place in China for the last five years because of the efforts of Chaiti Arts Foundation, an organization which manages to invite the best of Indian vocal and instrument musicians to functions held in Chinese cities.

Founded by two Shanghai-based business executives, Siddarth Sinha and Ravi Shankar Bose, Chaiti invites artists from India and hosts music programmes in five cities. The programme has been a journey of patience from the initial days—from a trickle at first to house-full shows today, with a visible Chinese presence.

Chinese interest in Indian music is expected to grow because the Chinese find a deep connect with India with regard to the philosophical depth underlying good music. Classical Indian music adds to the cultural image of India crafted around the popularity of its food, music, yoga and Bollywood.

China now produces some of the best piano and violin players of Western classical music, indicating their ability to learn and adopt new forms of music.

'Introducing a completely new genre of music to the local audience was a path-breaking task. We took it as a responsibility,' said Siddharth Sinha, one of the two founders of Chaiti.

Chaiti found special recognition from major Chinese companies such as Huawei, China Eastern Airlines and C-trip, who have come forward to sponsor and support the cultural programmes it puts up to host visiting musicians from India. The new interest for Indian music among Chinese business is a significant pointer to the fact that they want to be associated with India for the long haul.

'Exchange of dialogue between artists of the two countries allows for an understanding of history and application of ragas. I believe something very special and great has survived between these cultures for thousands of years, and this needs to be nurtured. It must be celebrated in unison,' said Sinha.

According to Siddarth, the support Chaiti received from the Embassy of India, Consulate General of India in Shanghai and Guangzhou, the Indian Council for Cultural Relations and the Confederation of Indian Industry has gone a long way in strengthening Chaiti. Chaiti has also initiated musical engagements such as *baithaks* and workshops to encourage young Indian talent to interact and teach Chinese interested in Indian music. Some well-known Indian artistes have also flown in to teach at these workshops. This work adds to the efforts by the Indian embassy to teach music and dance.

Classical music is not expected to evoke feet-thumping popularity in any country, including India and China. But it has some significant contributions beyond the joys of music: It gives substance and prestige to a people's culture and connects with the elite in different countries. This is why ministers, high officials and business leaders attend music events either as a much-needed break from political and business cacophony or because they want to be counted among the cultural elite.

The 'democracy' of TikTok and WeChat

China's global influencers are in Internet and mobile platforms and in forms like the video dissemination app TikTok, the chatting app WeChat and the YouTube clone YouKu, and several e-commerce sites. The first two have become hugely popular in India.

It's curious that China, which has banned YouTube and Facebook, besides several Indian media, is connecting with millions of Indians through these Internet platforms. One hardly hears protests from the government for banning Indian sites.

Many Indians have begun to use WeChat along with WhatsApp because of its strong video-chatting facility. WeChat is also a payment platform allowing people in China to buy things, but it is unlikely that the Reserve Bank of India would give it the necessary licence to perform this kind of limited banking.

TikTok, the video platform, is doing for China what Bollywood has done for India. Their impact on image-building exceeds that of the official publicity departments and formal media. It is hugely popular in India, the US and dozens of other countries.

Positioning itself as 'Real people. Real Videos', TikTok provides a fun-filled, troll-free Internet environment. It has managed to involve millions of teenagers, besides ordinary folks like security guards, construction workers and, quite often, housewives.

'TikTok is more than entertainment. It is helping the world see "Asians" and "Chinese" in a new light,' said Saurabh Sharma, UX strategist and researcher based in Los Angeles. 'TikTok could well do for the East what Hollywood did for the West.'

Users of the platform are aware that it is a Chinese mobile app, and this adds to the image of China as a producer of innovative products. One sees videos of tourist destinations and awesome infrastructure in China. It also helps spread the message that the Chinese are friendly and fun-loving people.

An important question is whether TikTok is helping the growth of other Chinese brands.

'I don't think it helps the established Chinese brands. But Chinese manufacturers of unbranded products (like duck-tape makers) use the platform to demonstrate their products,' Sharma said.

11

THE TRUMP EFFECTS

US President Donald Trump may have his reasons for initiating measures that that could culminate in a mutually destructive trade war with China, but the emerging situation is also throwing up opportunities for new players.

When Donald Trump became president of the United States in January 2017, no one really thought his election rhetoric about China stealing American jobs would snowball into a corrosive trade war. In his third year as president, Trump is as relentless in his attacks on China as he had been earlier although there are signs that he may be contemplating concessions on a few issues like the ban on Huawei Technologies.[1]

Since July 2018, the two countries have been engaged in a tit-for-tat tariff war that has already resulted in losses worth billions of dollars to businesses across the globe. The two sides have already held ten rounds of intense talks for a peace deal to end the trade war, but the situation has only worsened.

Can India benefit from the trade war?

'Yes indeed, it is an opportunity. Studies show that the China–US trade war gives further opportunities of export in several items such as vegetables, minerals, leather and leather products, textiles and clothing, metals and transportation,' Prabir De, professor at and coordinator of the ASEAN-India Centre at the Research and Information System for Developing Countries (RIS), told me in an interview.

Like many other countries, India is not insulated from the US–China trade war. There were some who thought US President Donald Trump would take forward the campaign to corner China in the trade front by encouraging India to play a bigger role.

Some would have expected US President Donald Trump to encourage Indian exports at a time when he is putting tremendous pressure on China on the trade front. Instead, he decided to remove India from the Generalized System of Preferences (GSP), effective 5 June 2019, which allowed a significant quantity of Indian products and services to flow into the US without paying any duty. The duty advantage which India enjoyed along with its developing country status for three decades has now vanished.

The White House said that the president had 'determined that India has not assured the United States that India will provide equitable and reasonable access to its markets'. Trump later went ahead and did the same thing with Turkey.

In effect, this means that US importers of Indian goods and services will be required to pay more than USD 300 million a year in new duties. This might hit Indian exports to the US. Earlier, the preferential trade treatment for India under the GSP allowed close to USD 5.6 billion worth of exports to enter the US duty-free.

India responded by saying Washington's decision would have 'minimal economic impact'. India also decided to go on the counter-offensive with the US, raising duties on imports from USA after its GSP decision.

'This is a domino effect—retaliation on reciprocity,' De said. 'But India is not raising tariffs too much except on a few items. Increasing tariff wouldn't help Indian production as most of the country's export sector depends very much on imported parts and components,' he said.

The solution lies in de-escalating the trade war and restore the process of globalization, which has suffered some serious setbacks. Is Washington or Beijing listening? Very unlikely because new issues touching on security and China's core issue of Taiwan has got linked in its trade war with the US.

For India, the question is whether intense pressure from the United States and rising resistance in European Union countries—the two biggest trade partners for China—are going to nudge Chinese companies to move their industrial capacities and invest more in India.

China has been shifting its industrial capacity of Vietnam,[2] Indonesia and other countries long before the trade war begun because it wants to clean up pollution factories and find new avenues for businesses that cannot afford rising land and labour costs at home. Besides, technologies have changed, and companies saddled with old ones are looking for markets where they can be used. The shift did not take place in India because it is geographically far without a proper land route, and also because of political uncertainties. Will the trade war change the situation?

There are signs this is happening at a small scale and limited to Chinese companies who see significant opportunities in the Indian market as they are fearful of losing their businesses in the US.

Of late, US President Donald Trump has also begun tightening the screws on India, by not just reducing the number of work visas the US can grant to Indian citizens but also planning to take away the duty-free status for a section of Indian exports. If Chinese companies plan to avoid the 'Made in China' stamping by making goods in India for markets in the US, this may not be possible because Trump is taking some aggressive steps towards India as well. At least, this could be an argument against using India as a base for Chinese production.

Tony Zhao, chairman of Blue Carbon Technology, based in China's Shandong province, is confident that India could be a good manufacturing and export base for his company making solar power-based lighting and refrigeration equipment. The company is building two plants in India.

'Even if the US is putting some pressure on India, the situation is not the same as with China. Anything made in India will face much less resistance than when it is made in China in these days of a trade war,' the company's sales director Daina Zhu said.

Trump's main grouse against China is that it is sitting on a USD 350 billion trade deficit. India is in no such situation and cannot attract his bitterness with the same intensity.

China's woes

The US decision disallowing Huawei to sell products or source technology in the country is what has put the Chinese government in a worse bind. It can handle some increases in taxes on Chinese exports although Trump's decision to penalize USD 200 billion worth of Chinese goods with higher tariff and the threat of covering another USD 300 billion of such products is already having a damaging effect on the country's industrial climate as a whole.

But what worries Zhongnan Hai, the fortress-like complex in Beijing that shields government ministers and officials from ordinary eyes out in the street, is the fear that Trump's moves against China's technology acquisition from the US would severely harm its plans for overall upgradation of the industrial process. Beijing has particularly been riding high on the strength of 5G technology of Huawei, which is believed to be ahead of all companies in the field. US aggression towards Chinese business goes far beyond trade and covers areas like controls on technology transfer, enhanced scrutiny of Chinese investments and even an effort to restrict China-based companies to list in US stock exchanges. Beijing also fears the snowballing effect on its business dealings with Europe and development of its military capabilities which are increasingly been driven by high technology, including drones, robotics and AI.

Huawei's 5G technology will not only open doors for China to the Western world—which is still anxious and suspicious of Chinese motives—but also help power IoT, or the Internet of Things, robotics and all sorts of data-driven automation, which can change lives and help China get out of the 'middle-income trap' in which it finds itself.

At one stage Trump posted a tweet[3] saying he would increase tariffs on USD 200 billion worth of Chinese goods from 10 per cent to 25 per cent. This tweet, posted last May, signalled a reversal of a decision Washington took last February in the midst of trade talks to keep it at 10 per cent.

The tweet felt like a whiplash in Beijing, which immediately dispatched officials to Washington to talk things over. China is always trying to understand how it can placate Trump and soften his stance.

'The tweet is a big wrench in China's foreign trade policy,' said Nick Marro, an analyst at the Economist Intelligence Unit (EIU).

A worried Chinese foreign ministry responded saying, 'What is of vital importance is that we still hope the United States can work hard with China to meet each other halfway and strive to reach a mutually beneficial, win-win agreement on the basis of mutual respect.'

But some experts do not think there is a need to press the panic button. Shanghai-based expert Shen Dingli said, 'China and the US have big and overlapping stakes in bilateral trade. They will overcome any difficulties for a successful outcome of the trade talks.'[4]

'America does not have a propaganda department like the Chinese government. Therefore, Trump has invented something that is good for him,' Dingli said. 'A competent propaganda department has made China powerful. My president does not need to use his own account in WeChat (Chinese social media app) to communicate,' he said.

Washington and Beijing have engaged in reciprocal tariff hikes over the last year while negotiators have engaged in lengthy trade talks, alternating negotiations between the two capitals.

But China's retaliatory measures against the United States in their ongoing trade war have raised questions about the limitations of Beijing's ability to fight back.

Beijing's retaliation did not match the size of Washington's action of raising the tariff on USD 200 billion worth of Chinese goods from 10 per cent to 25 per cent. China has imposed additional taxes on a wide range of American goods worth USD 60 billion.[5] But Beijing has left out some crucial goods from enhanced taxation. They include technology-related products and farm commodities like soybean.

Most of the American products covered by additional taxation will see tariffs rising to 15–20 per cent while only a few will be taxed at 25 per cent.

But China is showing its muscle in other ways. Chinese buyers are cutting back on imports of American pork to the extent of USD 6.5 billion. This step will severely hit US pork farmers because China is the second-biggest importer of American pork.

Few expected China to take this measure at a time when its domestic pig farms have been hit by African swine fever. Some reports said Chinese pig breeders are at risk of losing one-third of their livestock.

'As a result of the African swine flu outbreak in China, the supply of pork has been affected. In April, pork prices surged by 14.4 per cent. To push down prices, China will need to import more pork,' Max Zenglein, head of economic research at the Mercator Institute for China Studies (MERICS) in Berlin, told me in an interview in May 2019.

China's Communist leaders are gauging the extent of sacrifices that Chinese consumers are willing to make at a time when the country is engaged in a bitter trade war, analysts said.

But it is in no mood to take chances with the supply of crucial American technology, which is essential for the survival and growth of hundreds of Chinese companies and joint ventures involving local and US firms.

This is why Beijing has spared many technology-related products in its decision to impose further taxes. Additionally, the government has offered exemptions to Chinese companies that cannot afford increased tariffs on essential imports.

China may have limited capability for tit-for-tat taxing of US goods, but it has other equally stronger ways of pressuring Washington. One of them is its ability to get the Chinese public to adhere to what the authorities want, even if they have to reduce purchases of highly taxed American goods.

'China doesn't have to reduce demand for foreign products through tariffs. It can simply direct that purchases be stopped,' said Doug Barry, an executive with US-China Business Council.[6]

'Although China imports less from the US, American companies are heavily invested in the market and generate significant profits there. This gives China considerable leverage,' Zenglein of MERICS said.

Beijing may put pressure on American businesses operating in China by cutting back on its buying of US products. Beijing recently moved away from buying US-made Boeing aircraft after a couple of tragic accidents and enhanced its purchase of Airbus jets made in France.

'China also has non-tariff options for making life distressing for US business people, such as more frequent inspections, costly audits, national security reviews and other forms of harassment,' Barry said.

The US industry is heavily dependent on Chinese manufacturers for a wide range of goods and parts, which cannot be easily substituted by supplies from other countries. Chinese companies are accustomed to the requirements of American users after decades of mutual dealings—something other markets cannot learn in a hurry, he said.

The question remains, however, about whether Beijing would use this as leverage because cutting off supplies from China would hurt its companies and cause large-scale disruptions and unemployment.

Political onslaught

One aspect of the trade war that has been given less attention is the threat it could pose to the ruling Communist Party of China (CPC).

If and when the US and China reach a settlement, China's communist leaders will find it extremely difficult to convince party cadres, local industries and even the public of the merits of the agreement.

The trade war is seen more as an attempt by Washington to force Beijing to accept an unequal deal. The Chinese media has painted a different picture portraying the US as a bully that is trying to contain a rising competitor.

'It sounds like the US is trying to impose an unequal treaty on China, which reminds many in China of the "Century of Humiliation" when the declining Qing Dynasty had to accept unequal treaties imposed on China by foreign powers,' said Zhiqun Zhu,[7] a political science professor at Bucknell University. And, accepting something that is perceived as an unequal treaty would be seen in China as a sign of weakness.

'I think it will be politically dangerous if the CPC does not put up a strong resistance (to Washington) and seek a fairer deal with the US,' Zhu said.

For the rank and file of China's Communist cadres, there is an expectation that the Chinese leadership will match up to the US in both political strength and negotiation capability. Some even see the trade war as a tussle between the two presidents, Xi Jinping and Donald Trump.

'The US's demand that China genuinely move towards a market economy is a challenge for any CCP leadership, but is particularly the case for a China led by Xi Jinping,' said Scott Kennedy,[8] deputy director of Freeman Chair in China Studies at the Center for Strategic and International Studies. According to him, that is equally challenging because under Xi Jinping's leadership China has moved backwards in terms of market reforms. He said, 'Previous CCP leaders have adopted policies less inimical to markets, and they did not see marketization as a vital threat to CCP rule the way Xi Jinping apparently does.'

Reports from the US suggest that Washington wants to craft the deal in a way that China cannot deviate from it or have any room for counter-measures such as tariff hikes on American business.

The Trump administration has imposed tariffs worth hundreds of billions of dollars on Chinese goods. Washington appears to be negotiating from a position of strength as China has exhausted its ability to impose counter-tariffs on American products.

The US is now asking China to address old concerns like industrial subsidies, technology transfer and intellectual property rights. Accepting these demands would impose a heavy financial burden on Chinese industry because it will result in costly restructuring and an increase in product prices. Price increases can, in turn, affect China's exports.

Questions are being asked about whether the US will find a way to make sure that the deal once signed is implemented at the factory and trade levels across China.

Deal or no deal, the situation in China is unlikely to change, said Fraser Howie, author of the book *Red Capitalism*.

'China will pay lip service to much of what is being discussed, sign a weak deal, buy some stuff, approve some deals in the short term but in the long term China will be pursuing Made in China 2025; they will be stealing IP where they can, and they will be treating foreign companies differently as much as they can,' he said.

Is China using trade was as pretext to enhance control over industry?

We need to examine if the colossal impact of Donald Trump's decisions and threatened moves on the Chinese industry would impact the Indian market as well.

One area of concern for foreign companies, including Indian ones, is whether the government under Xi Jinping is trying to extort control over the private sector which has seen tremendous growth, outstripping the most optimistic projections, simply because their boards were free to determine the corporate directions. Is that changing now?

In September 2018, Alibaba chairman Jack Ma's announced that he would step down as head of the world's biggest e-commerce company within one year. This has sparked animated discussions on whether the Chinese government was behind the decision.

Analysts are asking if the government is keen to enhance its influence over global giants from China like Huawei and the so-called BAT club of Baidu, Alibaba and Tencent. A change in government policy along this line will leave little space for high-profile and largely independent players like Jack Ma.

'The Chinese government seems to be wanting to have a more direct "say" in BAT, particularly in Alibaba and Tencent,' said Lourdes Casanova, director of Emerging Markets Institute at Cornell.[9] 'The government is saying, "You have become so powerful because we have protected you against the big world players. It is time to give us back",' she said, trying to analyse the government's viewpoint.

Beijing may have its constraints and the necessity to strengthen its economic diplomacy at a time when it faces severe trade challenges from the Trump administration in the United States. The government may want to control the direction of Chinese companies facing challenges in the US.

Jacob Cooke, CEO of consulting firm Web Presence in China, said, 'Ma is basically moving away from the company's chairmanship and might become a Chinese version of Warren Buffet making portfolio investments globally.'[10]

How will such a move impact India where Chinese companies have emerged as major investors?

Alibaba and the telecom giant Huawei Technologies are active in the Indian market through different investments while several Chinese companies like Xiaomi dominate the mobile phone market in India. Some would say, perhaps less charitably, that Beijing would be able to influence the directions of Chinese companies in India and thereby exert influence on the Indian market in a less evident manner.

Chinese companies established in world markets are a vital part of Beijing's economic diplomacy. They cut significant deals in different countries timed with the visit of country's leaders like its President Xi Jinping to foreign countries.

How are Chinese companies reworking their growth plans given the Trump challenge?

'Chinese companies are looking more at non-US markets and companies now. So India, South East Asia and Europe are getting more attention as markets. India and Indonesia probably offer the largest opportunities. However, most of the attention is still on China as that is the biggest opportunity for most companies,' said Jeffrey Towson, author and professor at the Peking University.

'In terms of acquiring technology, you see more attention to places like Israel, Japan and parts of Europe,' he said.

According to a June 2019 McKinsey report, there is no reason to believe that the trade war is leading to a major economic slowdown in China as reports in the media about the US–China tangles would suggest. US politicians have used these reports to show that their actions against China are having an effect.

The think tank said China's GDP is far less dependent on trade today than what some would have us believe. China's net trade surplus was only 1.7 per cent of GDP in 2017, down from 8 per cent in 2008.

The worst that trade sanctions can do to China has to do with chipping off a part of the surplus of 1.7 per cent of GDP, which might at most come down to 1 per cent of GDP. Even that much effect is doubtful as the Trump administration has come to realize that hitting China will come home to hit American consumers, particularly the vast population hungering for cheap Chinese products.

The effect may be more indirect, impacting consumer confidence and causing private sector companies to hold off on making decisions to invest in a more manufacturing capacity.

American CEOs like Elon Musk of Tesla have begun to complain they cannot make affordable goods without Chinese help. India and Vietnam might have low labour costs and land rentals, but they do not have the network of manufacturing capabilities, each feeding into another, unit after unit, cluster after cluster, in a smooth chain, that China has developed.

'Tesla was unable to source manufacturing for Autopilot 3.0 ECU in the United States,' Tesla told the US government. 'We turned to industry experts who could achieve this quality and complexity in addition to the deadlines, which was not possible outside of China,' it said.[11]

How China plans to overtake the US in technology

China's plans to become a leader in advanced industries and technologies, backed by massive subsidies and loans, among other measures, has left Western industrialized countries in a state of panic.

On the face of it, China Manufacturing 2025 or CM2025, launched four years ago, has laudable initiatives. But the differences between China's plans and similar strategies of the industrialized and other nations are causing concern. For one, China's planners have taken it upon themselves to steer the development of industries that they believe will drive the economy, thus ruling out market forces. More alarming are the subsidies—running into hundreds of billions in euros—loans and other channels of support and allegations that Chinese companies are simply stealing technology or arm-twisting foreign partners to part with technology. At the end of it, Chinese companies could be dominating not only their home market but also international markets, if CM2025 succeeds.

In 2015, even before Beijing announced CM2025, China was already an industrial powerhouse, as the European Chamber of Commerce in China has noted in an analytical report, 'China Manufacturing 2025'.[12]

In that year, China produced or assembled 28 per cent of the world's automobiles, 41 per cent of the world's ships, 80 per cent of the world's computers, 90 per cent of the world's mobile phones and 80 per cent of the world's air-conditioners, among others.

But Beijing had realized by then that much of this production has very little value-addition and at the same time is polluting and energy-intensive. So, it decided to upgrade its industrial base and compete in more advanced market segments. This would help China break into the high-income status and avoid getting trapped in the so-called middle-income zone.

At the same time, Chinese companies in high-tech sectors such as aerospace, machine tools, or software engineering are trying to catch up with foreign competitors by merely narrowing the technology gaps via transfers and not by spending more on R&D. In even more emerging sectors such as smart manufacturing, China wants to leapfrog and leave foreign competitors behind. In some industries, it reckons it can lead right from the word go.

China has already forged ahead in new-generation IT, high-speed railways and ultra-high voltage electricity transmissions. More than 530 smart manufacturing industrial parks have popped up in China. Many people focus on big data (21 per cent, new materials (17 per cent) and cloud computing (13 per cent).

China also has a strong position in areas such as artificial intelligence (AI), new energy and batteries for electric vehicles (EVs). In 2017, the European Chamber noted, seven of the top ten EV battery companies were Chinese, accounting for 53 per cent of the global market share. The expansion of China's battery manufacturing capacities is in the pipeline and could amount to three times that planned in the rest of the world.

The Made in China 2025 has sparked off fierce controversies and prompted the US and European countries to find ways of resisting it. 'In Western industrialized countries, China's ambition has caused considerable irritation. Businesses and experts assessed that China was using unfair business practices and stealing technology in its efforts to become the world's tech superpower,' MERICS, the Berlin-based think tank said in a report. 'MIC25 has fuelled concerns that foreign competitors would be pushed out of the lucrative Chinese market and face fierce competition in third world markets, while

China becomes not only more competitive in innovative sectors of its own domestic economy, but also as the market shares of Chinese companies abroad grow,' it said.

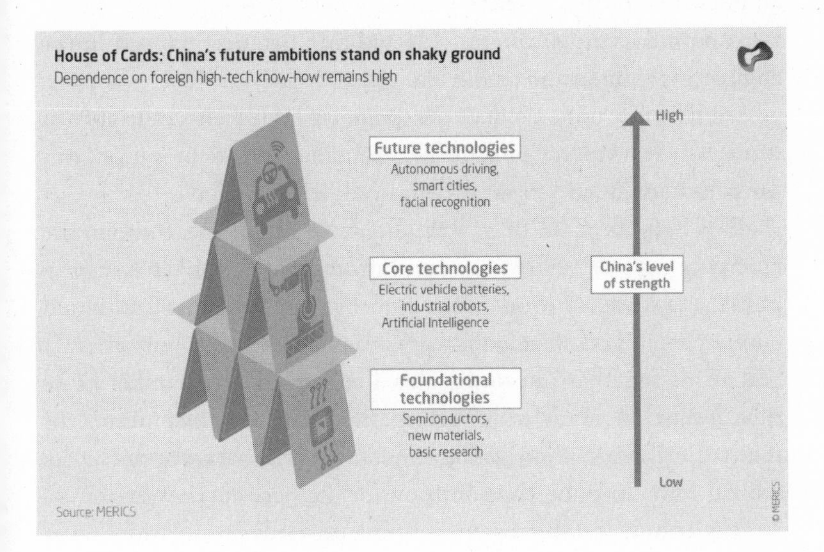

What were China's compulsions in adopting CM2025? In the last decade, China's growth has continuously slowed, and the economy's expansion in 2018 was just 6.6 per cent, the weakest since 1990. The country also risks being caught in the middle-income trap, a problem many developing countries faced when rising wages eroded their comparative advantage, making them unable to compete with the productivity and innovation of advanced economies.

While China's investments in R&D have been growing, and it is pushing its industry to improve quality and efficiency, foreign companies have issues with the policy tools that Beijing has deployed. The European Chamber says European business has facing intense pressure to turn over advanced technology in exchange for near-term market access while, in industrial robotics, government subsidies are contributing to overcapacity in the low- and mid-tiers of China's market.

CM2025 has created attractive opportunities for some European businesses to play an essential role in the short term, but the fear is that the market for European enterprises will shrink since it is mostly an import-substitution plan.

Another compulsion for CM2025 is demographics. China's eligible workforce, or those in the 15–59-year age group, is contracting. So, not only does the declining rate of economic growth mean that future development has to be driven by innovation, but the country will have to support more elderly citizens.

For China, CM2025 will also help it play a role in the emerging fourth industrial revolution, which will see cyber-physical systems of production controlled by big data and cloud computing, 'as connected networks of humans and robots interact and work together', according to the European Chamber. The first industrial revolution was sparked by the development of mechanical production driven by water and steam power, the second revolution by the adoption of mass production driven by electricity and the third was the move towards automation based on electronics and IT.

Many European companies in industries covered by CM2025, e.g., those in the rail industry, have seen market access become increasingly difficult as Chinese firms close the technological gap via mandated technology transfers from foreign companies, improve their internal R&D efforts and get preferential access to China's vast domestic market.

Despite these challenges, though, there are significant opportunities for European business. At least in the near to medium term, European companies that provide advanced capital equipment, as well as critical components and technologies that China is not yet able to produce itself, stand to benefit.

In some fields, European business can benefit from using their facilities in China to do contract manufacturing and R&D for domestic firms. In others, they can secure new business by providing components, services and expertise to state-owned enterprises or

SOEs and private Chinese firms that are doing projects relevant to CM2025 in third-party markets.

Service providers that can assist Chinese firms in integrating industrial robotics, sensors and advanced software systems into their assembly lines also stand to gain. The government's priorities may also produce new opportunities for testing, inspection and certification (TIC) companies.

The European Chamber has studied the outlook by industry, with specific reference to five of the ten sectors covered by CM2025:

1. Next-generation IT (including cloud computing, telecommunications equipment and semiconductors)
2. Robotics
3. Advanced rail equipment
4. Energy-saving vehicles and New Energy Vehicles (NEVs)
5. Biopharmaceuticals and high-performance medical devices

In next-generation IT, the concern is that China is attempting to nationalize many aspects of its IT industry by substituting products manufactured by foreign investment enterprises (FIEs) with indigenous technology that is 'secure and controllable'.

In cloud computing, the concern is that limitations on European business' access to China's cloud computing market for the Infrastructure as a Service (IaaS) and Platform as a Service (PaaS) segments have been formalized, and European business remains unable to attain the Internet Data Centre (IDC) licence. This limits the ability of European companies operating in China to choose the service provider most aligned with their needs. Furthermore, requirements that cloud service operators locate their service facilities and network data within Chinese territory are likely to hamper entrepreneurship and prevent innovative products and services from being created or adopted within the country.

In telecommunications equipment, the concern is that the level of export credits that leading Chinese telecommunications equipment manufacturers receive from government agencies allow them to win contracts in international markets based on price, which runs the risk of depressing innovation in the industry globally.

In semiconductors, the concern is that, by attempting to upgrade the technological capabilities of its domestic semiconductor industry with support from enormous, government-backed investment funds at the central, provincial and city level, China risks creating overcapacity, which could depress profit margins and technological development in the global industry.

The government-driven scheme to acquire controlling stakes in international semiconductor companies and technologies is also highly troubling. Given that these are areas where European business is barred from making equivalent investments in China, it runs the risk of provoking a push-back from abroad, which will diminish the exposure to the international industry that China needs to develop its capabilities.

In robotics, serious overcapacity is emerging in the low and mid-tiers of the industrial robotics market, largely as a result of government subsidies.

In NEVs, in a move that contravenes China's WTO obligations, European business is being pressured to transfer core technology in exchange for near-term market access. Further, foreign companies face serious constraints on market access for NEV batteries, and a high percentage of the subsidies that the central and local authorities have provided to the industry have been directed to favoured domestic companies that often lack strong technological capacity.

In advanced rail equipment, the concern for Western companies is that discrimination against FIEs has increased in procurement for rail contracts and market access has continued to decrease.

In medical devices, the concern is that, at the highest political level, a directive to 'nationalize' China's medical device industry has been publicly delivered. This has resulted in many instances of medical devices produced by European companies being prevented from competing for public procurement contracts on a level playing field, and often includes devices manufactured in China by European companies. This limits choice in the market and prevents hospitals from the critical task of purchasing equipment that is best suited to meeting the clinical needs of patients.

A fundamental challenge China faces is a lack of the advanced workforce skills needed to succeed with CM2025. China does not have reliable data on employment, and there are skills and labour market issues that could sink CM2025. While automation also results in new types of jobs, it is not clear whether the government understands the impact that this shift in employment will have.

The significance of this potential shift is highlighted by a 2015 study by Boston Consulting Group,[13] which found that over the next decade in Germany—a country with a far more mature vocational education system—Industry 4.0 would lead to the loss of 610,000 jobs and the creation of 960,000 new ones in fields like analytics, R&D and new positions resulting from revenue growth opportunities. China's vocational educational system needs to prepare for exactly this kind of scenario.

China has plenty of talented software engineers, but there is a danger that the top companies in a given industry will exhaust the pool of skilled workers, leaving none for smaller companies to employ. A 2015 survey of more than 2000 China-based employers with a total of four million employees has highlighted this issue. Nearly half the respondents said a severe skills shortage had the potential to hit effective operations.

This is a serious problem since talent is the top driver of manufacturing competitiveness, followed by cost competitiveness and productivity.

However, China has announced plans to reform and upgrade its vocational education system, with a target of enrolling 23.5 million students in secondary vocational schools and 14.8 million in two-year, college-level vocational schools by 2020. The downside is the relevance of the training at the vocational institutions.

Without skilled labour, it will prove difficult for China to effectively compete based on quality. For example, without enough skilled workers to maintain industrial robots, the value that robots can contribute to manufacturing lines will quickly be lost. Also, as China struggles to create millions of new jobs every year, industrial automation will disturb social equality and stability.

Earlier, when China directed subsidies towards developing industries, the result was overcapacity. This is already an issue for industrial robotics. According to the European Chamber, before China's technological and manufacturing industries can reach their full potential, the authorities need to move forward with market-based reforms. Facilitating a competitive environment for private enterprises, allowing market forces to reign and creating strong political institutions will ultimately prove more effective at driving economic development and innovation than efforts by government officials to steer capital and support into industries that they have identified as priorities through a top-down process.

China has been one of the leading beneficiaries of the open, liberal trading order since it opened up forty years ago, but its benefits are under strain in the current backlash against free trade and globalization sparked by politicians who are against free trade politicians in many countries around the world. Here, China is already seen as a cause of the problems faced by national economies elsewhere.

Today, it is essential for China to grant more market access to foreign companies and investors, while European Union members must cite their benefits from trade relations with China.

In this anti-free-trade world, China should help in developing new international investment guidelines that will ensure that the legitimate interests of all countries are given due consideration. Regular commercial transactions should not be unnecessarily politicized, and China should heed the requirements of foreign investors.

Chinese planners are engaging on several levels to eliminate the weaknesses in its grand plan. It has been investing heavily in research. The European Chamber says China spent around USD 300 billion on research and development, nearly 2.2 per cent of GDP.[14] Sheer scale in absolute figures might, at some point, give China an advantage over smaller industrialized countries that spend much less. As a percentage of GDP, China's R&D spending has already surpassed that of the EU (2.1 per cent).

Second, the government is pushing to more centrally coordinate the implementation of its MIC25 or Made in China 2025 policy and related industrial policies. Unlike previous national economic policy plans, MIC25 attaches more importance to private companies, entrepreneurship and market mechanisms while at the same time improving the competitiveness of state-owned enterprises that are still considered crucial for the innovation drive. In the eyes of China's leadership, this is part of an effort to optimize China's hybrid state capitalist system. But many contradictions associated with simultaneously strengthening market forces and the role of the state remain unresolved.

12

CONCLUSION: THE PATH AHEAD

We have looked at the entire breadth of business relations between India and China from more than a dozen different angles and listened to experts and businessmen engaged in the daily struggle for profit.

Many Indian companies have the opportunity to grow dramatically if they find creative ways to adopt new technologies while operating in China and engaging with Chinese companies in India and in other countries. It is also wise to engage with a potential competitor before he overtakes our business as we have seen in market segments like mobile phones and some parts of the whitegoods market.

'Indian industry can certainly take advantage of rising Chinese investments in India,' Chandrajit Banerjee, director general of CII, told me in an interview. 'I believe there is huge potential and scope for more Chinese companies to invest and operate in India in a range of different sectors,' he said.

Banerjee also said, 'The Chinese are signalling their readiness to address some of India's market access concerns in the context of burgeoning adverse trade balance of India.'

China is a market for the long-distance runner, and those seeking quick profits, do not expect to establish a toehold in it. But those that enter the market with determination and make efforts to communicate with the local business can reap huge benefits.

A compelling case is that of the Vinmart Group, owned by Gujarati businessmen who, among other things, source cobalt from the Republic of Congo in Africa and sell it in China. This is significant because China is the world's biggest user of cobalt and Chinese businessmen own a significant number of cobalt mines in Congo.

'The key to survival in China's business scene is price competitiveness, relationships, reputation and product quality,' Rushi Chug, director of Vinmart Group told me at his office in the south Chinese city of Guangzhou.

Chug also said, 'Long-term relationship with Chinese business partners helps in the sense that you don't have to prove again and again that you are a genuine supplier or buyer and your reputation is upheld.'

Some Indian companies have already realized the business potential for China for themselves. A recent survey by Confederation of Indian Industry and Evalueserve showed that 30 per cent of Indian companies based in China generated more than 10 per cent of their global revenue from China. About 80 per cent of the Indian firms in the consumer goods sector told surveyors that their China operations contributed 10 per cent of their global revenue.

About 39 per cent of the companies surveyed said they plan to invest more in China in 2019 than they did in 2018.

Several Chinese executives have told me that their main challenge in India is the government red tape which involves obtaining several licences and getting elaborate documentation done in state capitals and districts. It's also challenging for them to find suitable Indian partners. The problematic issues are inadequate communication and differences in management systems of the Indians and the Chinese.

When it comes to investing, the Chinese have shown a preference for India's digital and telecommunications sectors while leaving out the vast industrial manufacturing, including automobile sectors.

Chinese companies should consider entering into manufacturing of car batteries and electronics because India is going for electric vehicles in a big way, Maruti Suzuki India chairman R.C.Bhargave told me. They have little presence in India's automobile sector, partly because the Chinese manufacturers are primarily focused on big cars and India is a small-car market, he said.

The Chinese may emerge as important players and even begin to move the Indian stock market in the coming months. At least two delegations of Chinese stock investors have visited Mumbai and met Indian brokers and institutional investors in 2019. There is a vast corpus of investible funds with Chinese companies because investment opportunities for them in China and the Western world is shrinking. What they want to make sure is the legal route for bringing in investments and repatriating profits. Though this may be a lucrative and useful option for Indian companies, there is a risk of sudden withdrawal of funds from the market if and when there is a political dispute between India and China.

Prime Minister Narendra Modi's announcement about a USD1.4 trillion (Rs 100 trillion) infrastructure development plan and the government's overall objective to making India a USD 5 trillion economy by 2024 has been heard loud and clear in Beijing. China is looking for investing destinations at a time when Western countries are imposing restrictions on Chinese forays.

With S. Jaishankar taking over as external affairs minister after serving as ambassador in China and the US, the government's ability to manoeuvre and take a realistic view of the relationship has substantially improved. Beijing is unlikely to sacrifice its political objectives concerning Pakistan, particularly in a situation where India refuses to adopt its ambitious Belt and Road Initiative.

But its need for the Indian market has grown more intense with US President Donald Trump imposing new restrictions on US–China trade. Can India manage to lure in American investments that were initially meant for China owing to the trade war with the US?

The recent government decision widening the scope of foreign direct investments (FDI) to 100 per cent in several sectors is partly aimed at taking advantage of the changing investment scenario at the international level. It is also a sign of desperation because the industrial investment is falling rapidly. At the same time, the government's decision to slash corporate tax will incentivize Chinese investments in India as much as it will Indian companies.

Indian officials are trying to see that happen, but they seem to have allowed many of the opportunities to slip by with Vietnam attracting most of such investments. One reason for Vietnam's attractiveness is that the Chinese have already built elaborate manufacturing infrastructure in that country. Chinese businesses had begun moving plants to Vietnam for over a decade to overcome problems like high wages and land prices besides restrictions on pollution in China.

It may be easier for India to attract Chinese investments instead of pinning a lot of hope on Americans diverting their investments from China to India. Many Chinese companies are desperately looking for not just markets but alternative production bases that are less expensive than in China.

Though India has allowed Huawei Technologies to carry out 5G trials, New Delhi may use it in its dealings with China. An important question is whether it will be used to apply political pressure or as a bargaining chip to secure concessions for Indian companies. Beijing is desperate to see the worldwide success of Huawei's 5G technology, and some Western countries are using the situation to achieve political goals. India is expected to go that way.

There has been a fascination about China's economic miracle, as some people describe it, in India. Way back in 2004, the then prime minister Manmohan Singh was quoted as saying that Mumbai has the potential to grow as much as Shanghai. The late Vilasrao Deshmukh, former Maharashtra chief minister, even promised to turn Mumbai into Shanghai.

China's economic decisions and their implementation continues to baffle foreigners, including Indians, more than forty years after it launched an 'opening up' programme and economic reforms with the then leader, Deng Xiaoping, giving a call to 'emancipate the mind'. He challenged the established idea of socialism to allow a selected group of people to become rich. 'Let some people get rich first,' Deng declared.

'Anything that China does is usually awe-inspiring and yet, for us in India, the understanding of how the world's second-largest economy really works, is superficial. In most cases, business leaders and even political think tanks have preconceived notions [about China] which prove to be a severe deterrent in moving forward,' Gagan Sabharwal, senior director, NASSCOM, told me.

Foreign governments and businessmen wonder how China plans and implements airport, rail and other projects years and decades ahead of any sign of emerging demand, besides encouraging the industry to implement grandiose plans without sufficient market surveys and projection of future demand.

But it must be understood that almost all the major construction companies in China are state-owned. The few private companies engaged in this business are mostly focused on housing construction and on conducting odd jobs that state-owned giants outsource. China's stunning growth in urbanization is driven by state finance, state management and state construction.

Most of the awesome success demonstrated by well-known Chinese companies like Alibaba, Huawei, Tencent, Baidu, DJI, Sunning and JD are in areas like information and communications technology (ICT), marketing and house construction.

At this time, China is building a new city called the Xiongan New Area, about 100 kms from Beijing, on a land area of 100 square kilometres, which can be doubled in size at a later date. It is implementing another project called the Greater Bay Area plan to connect the business and industrial hubs of Hong Kong, Shenzhen, Macau and Guangzhou in south China.

These two projects would cost several billion dollars, and would inject new momentum in the economy by pushing up demand for cement, steel, construction machinery and a host of other goods used to build cities. China has always used major projects as economic stimulus to generate demand and employment and eliminate the possibility of political revolt. There is even a suspicion that the Great Wall was financed, at least for some years, with this sort of motivation and not just to keep out the invaders.

Some economists view this as reckless investing and point to the fact that uncontrolled spending has resulted in the creation of ghost towns with full set of infrastructure and no humans living there, while building up a mountain of debt that the government is now grappling with. Western experts have been saying for several years that the heap of domestic debt, part of which has been built by shadow banks financing ill-conceived projects, is a ticking bomb which will bring down the Chinese economy. They said that the economic growth in China may just be 4 per cent a year, and not the official claim of 6.5 per cent, if the high level of debt and other negative factors are taken into account.

The fact that the Chinese ways have worked and resulted in a miracle does not make them perfect economic models that can be replicated by India or any other country. There are parallels to the industrial growth of Japan and South Korea, which preceded that of China. The situation has changed. The Chinese model has a lot to learn about, but it cannot be copied directly.

Another trend emerging from Beijing concerns 'military escort services' and 'military diplomacy' with Chinese characteristics. The idea is to allow Chinese navy and other services of the military to play an active role in different parts of the world under the guise of protecting Chinese goods and services and also Chinese citizens working in foreign countries. The process has already begun in the Gulf of Aden and in Pakistan, and is it likely to spread in other parts of the world.

India is closely watching the China Pakistan Economic Corridor, which is expected to give it a direct access to the Arabian Sea through the China-financed Gwadar project in Pakistan. The business implications of these developments are that overwhelming military presence creates political risks and results in conflicts with the US, and, in the future, even with India. In the uncertain future, such moves might impact Indian imports to different countries.

New and emerging trends

Let us look at the future trends in diverse fields of activity in China and examine how they will impact Indian conditions. Beijing's ambition must be kept in mind for a clearer understanding of the trends. What Chinese President Xi Jinping once called the 'China dream' has now turned into a determination to overtake the US as the world's biggest economy in GDP terms.

Despite the trade war and economic slowdown which has shrunk growth to 6.5 per cent of GDP, China has not entirely lost its 'factory the world' image and continues to manufacture for importers in India, the US and many other countries.

Indian companies will tell you they can see no alternative to Chinese products and machinery that go in the making of other goods. There is also a dependence on China for a large number of chemicals. Some of it may be substituted by emerging economies like Vietnam, and India itself, but the reliance on Chinese supplies will continue for the next several years.

Southern and eastern Chinese cities have built an ecosystem of manufacturers supporting each other with components and enhanced raw material that go into making the final product for any given industry. The ecosystem is largely missing in a wide range of Indian industry. In some cases, some of the 'connector' companies manufacturing essential components have closed down owing to competition from China.

Chinese manufacturers have their own problems. They face higher cost in terms of debt servicing, rising wages, land and raw material prices. Add to this, government crackdown on polluting factories and a sharp reduction in imports.

A new divergence in trend has now emerged with Chinese factories increasingly adapting robotics and the use of drones for manufacturing and logistics. There is a widespread use of computer automation, virtual testing and simulation in the production process. Besides, they are embracing globalized manufacturing to cater to changing consumer needs with as little a time lag as possible.

This is helping them produce in large quantities without the dependence on skilled labour. The government is supportive because it helps China battle the problem of an ageing population.

Incidentally, this has given rise to a huge demand for skilled engineers and hunger for importing talent. Several city governments in China, including Shanghai, are offering incentives for foreign talent. This trend is expected to result in a major flow of Indian engineers and specialists to China. A large number of Indian students engaged in post-doctoral studies are already engaged in research at Chinese universities and government-run laboratories.

Some Indian analysts have proposed that India take advantage of China's challenges and try to lure in Chinese companies eager to shift their low-technology, highly polluting industrial capacity. Vietnam has adopted this model quite successfully, partly because it is a land neighbour and able to provide Chinese culture and ecosystem to the new investors.

A large number of Indian companies are importing second-hand machinery from China, which are available at low prices. They make sense in some cases where the concerned Indian industry may be using technologies that are lower than the imported second-hand machinery. But if they result in regression to low-technology and high-pollution environment, such imports can be counter-productive.

The government needs to be aware of this possibility, and encourage institutions like the ISI to come up with specific standards to discourage the import of regressive technology.

Those in India proposing the Vietnam model for India are looking for a band-aid solution instead of a long-term one. India should use its scientific, IT and engineering talent to jump ahead in the manufacturing cycle and attract Chinese investments at a middle or higher level of technology, instead of retracing the steps to the era of polluting industries.

Another trend is towards increasing China's share of the world e-commerce market. It is expected to rise from USD 78 billion in 2016 to USD 140 billion by 2021 with Chinese players like Alibaba, Tencent and JD stretching out to different countries and even buying off foreign e-commerce companies partly or fully. This is evident in Chinese investments in Flipkart and Paytm in India.

India is considering the Chinese request for working towards a future free-trade agreement, allowing both countries to reduce or fully eliminate import tariff on goods from either country. Chinese companies which are promoting the idea of e-commerce free-trade zone in foreign countries will be the biggest beneficiary. New Delhi has to work out ways to allow Indian companies to take advantage of the situation before agreeing to the proposal.

As we have discussed earlier, China is effectively importing Internet platforms like WeChat for online chatting, TikTok for video dissemination and the YouTube clone, YouKu, to influence people across the globe. These platforms help create a positive image of China.

One might argue that Indian IT industry did not throw up such platforms because they faced competition from the American players. But the fact is that no serious effort has been made in the use of advanced algorithms for Internet platforms in India. Incidentally, Bollywood deserves kudos for its continued striving for technical excellence.

Competition is a powerful teacher. So is collaboration. Indian government and businesses must use both strategies in different areas to gain advantage. For instance, India has a lot to gain from technical cooperation with China to learn more about technologies like making clean coal, underground coal mining and environment-friendly mining, besides enhanced use of renewable energy and their distribution through stable grids. On its part, China is looking for contracts like the Chennai–Bangalore–Mysore railway upgradation project, training of Indian railway management staff, and, possibly, Delhi–Agra high-speed railway project.

Let's end with a parable attributed to Han Fei Zi (BCE 230), the Chinese philosopher who said that human beings give primacy to their self-interest above all else. The carriage maker hopes that men will grow rich and buy more carriages. The coffin maker would like to see more people dying for his business to grow. The carriage maker is not wishing good fortune for all, nor is the coffin maker thinking in evil terms. Both are only thinking about their own survival and growth.

Results of a survey of Indian companies in China released by CII and Evalueserve in August 2019

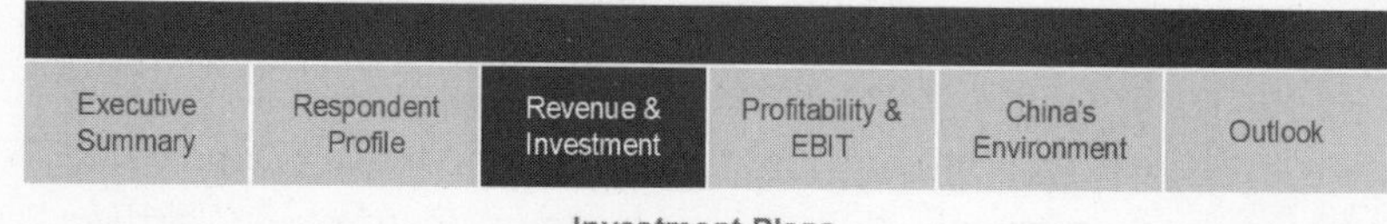

Investment Plans

Investment Plan for 2019

Q *How much investment have you planned for 2019 in China?*

More than 20%	11%, 6
Increase by 15%–20%	7%, 4
Increase by 10%–15%	4%, 2
Increase by 5%–10%	7%, 4
Increase by 1%–5%	11%, 6
Stay the same	60%, 34
Decrease or close operations	2%, 1

22 companies (39%) plan to invest more in 2019 than they did in 2018.

11% (6) plan to increase investment by more than 20%. Of these, 5 have >75% employees from mainland China.

Investment Plan by Sector

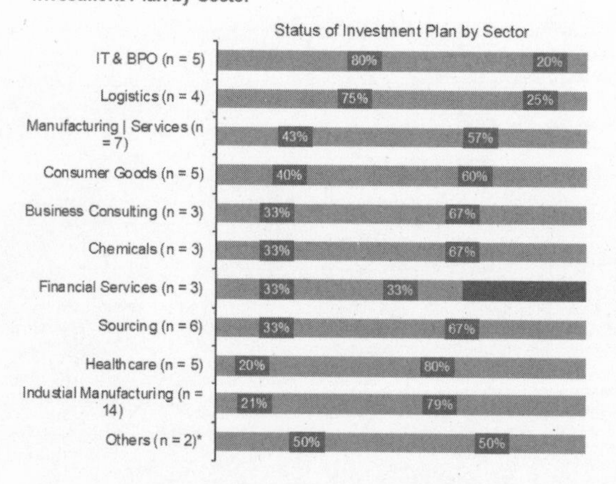

Over 50% of IT&BPO and Logistics companies are planning for additional investment in 2019. Only 1 company (in the Financial Services segment) has no plan to invest in 2019.

*Because the number of respondents within few industries was very low, therefore they have been counted as 'others' to maintain anonymity.

17

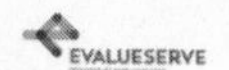

Executive Summary	Respondent Profile	Revenue & Investment	Profitability & EBIT	China's Environment	Outlook

Internal and External Challenges

Major External Challenges in China

Q *What are the greatest external challenges faced by your company in China (select 5)?*

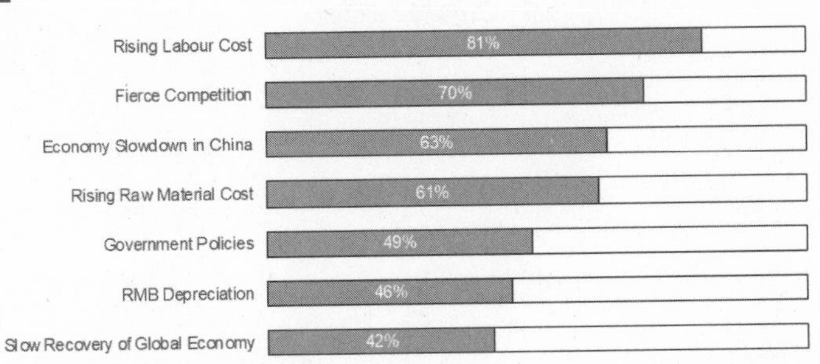

About 81% companies listed High Labour Cost as the primary external challenge. Of these, 31% had >150 employees in China.

More than 60% considered Competition, Economic Slowdown and Increasing Raw Material Cost as other external challenges.

Major Management Challenges in China

Q *What are the greatest management challenges faced by your company in China (select 5)?*

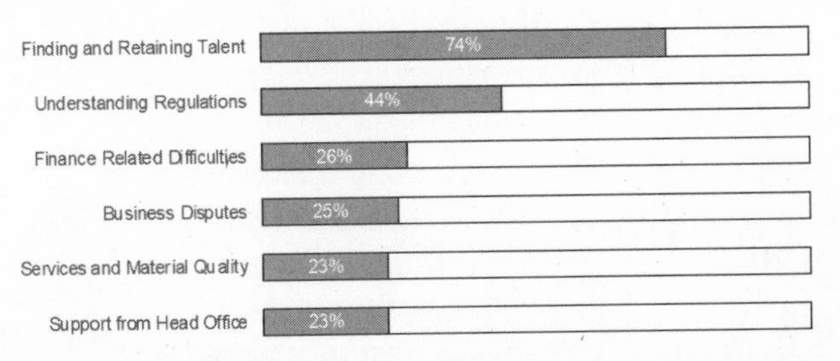

Around 74% respondents rated Finding and Retaining Talent as a management challenge, while 44% (25 companies) highlighted Understanding Regulation as a management challenge. However, among the latter group, 65% companies do not have a dedicated team for regulatory affairs.

Other key challenges include Financial Related Difficulties (26%), Business Disputes (25%) and Service and Material Quality (23%).

NOTES

Chapter 1: Tapping Opportunities

1. 'Foreign Minister Wang Yi Meets the Press', Embassy of the People's Republic of China, 9 March 2018.
2. 'China and the world: Inside the dynamics of a changing relationship', McKinsey Global Institute, July 2019 report, 7 July 2019.
3. Ibid.
4. 'India received $1.81 bn FDI from China during Apr '14- Mar '19: Piyush Goyal', the *Economic Times*, 28 June 2019.
5. Department for Promotion of Industry and Internal Trade of the Government of India, New Delhi.
6. Maulik Pathak and Elizabeth Roche, 'Xi Jinping, Narendra Modi get down to business in Gujarat', Livemint, 17 September 2014.
7. 'Fosun Pharma acquires 74% stake in Gland Pharma for $1.09 billion', the *Economic Times*, 4 October 2017.
8. 'Fosun Backed India's Logistic Unicorn Delhivery Raised USD 413mn in its Series F Financing', Fosun, 20 June 2019.
9. 'Foreign Minister Wang Yi Meets the Press', China's Ministry of Foreign Affairs, 9 March 2018.
10. N.S. Vageesh, 'Why are Indian banks curtailing overseas operations', *The Hindu BusinessLine*, 3 May 2018, https://bit.ly/2Zu1MAW.
11. Amanda Lee, 'China's state-owned companies enjoyed record profits, even as private sector flounders', *South China Morning Post*, 18 January 2019, https://bit.ly/2B1P2Uf
12. Benn Steil and Benjamin Della Rocca, 'China is heaping debt on its least productive companies', Center for Foreign Relations, 11 January 2018, https://on.cfr.org/2UdoW8Q

13. 'World in 2050: The long view: how will global economic order change by 2050', PricewaterhouseCoopers, 1 August 2019, https://pwc.to/2kl6hcQ

Chapter 2: Aiming High: 1000-strong Chinese Firms in India

1. 'India received $1.81 bn FDI from China during Apr'14- Mar'19: Piyush Goyal', the *Economic Times*, 28 June 2019, 11 June 2019, https://bit.ly/2NQtvoL
2. Pankaj Doval and Sujit John, 'China-US trade spat will lead to more Chinese investments into India: Xiaomi founder Lei Jun', the *Economic Times*, 14 May 2019, https://bit.ly/2ZB0TGi
3. Soumya Gupta, 'India's e-commerce market to hit $200 billion by 2026: Morgan Stanley report', Livemint, 13 October 2017, https://bit.ly/2TQCupi
4. 'India's digital future', Morgan Stanley, 12 October 2017, https://mgstn.ly/2yl1flY
5. Indian government and industry sources

Chapter 3: Collaboration Challenges

1. Supraja Srinivasan, 'China's Shunwei Capital raises $1.21 b for its latest global fund', the *Economic Times*, 5 November 2018, https://bit.ly/2Lbp1Y2

2. 'Tencent Holdings buys majority stake in gaming app Dream11 Fantasy', CNBC, 6 September 2018

Chapter 4: Doing Business in China

1. Zhang Ruimin, 'Why Haier Is Reorganizing Itself around the Internet of Things', Strategy+Business, 26 February 2018, https://bit.ly/2ZIO6h2

Chapter 6: Building Infrastructure and Influence

1. Bamber Gascoigne, *A Brief History of the Dynasties of China* (London: Robinson, 2003).

2. PTI, 'India will not accept project that violates its sovereignty: MEA on China's OBOR', the *Economic Times*, 5 April 2018, https://bit.ly/30RysRS
3. PTI, 'India to connect North East with Bangladesh's Chittagong port: Ram Madhav', Livemint, 15 August 2018, https://bit.ly/2PslIQ8
4. Liu Caiyu, 'Indian official's project invite deserves "cautious welcome": Chinese analysts,' *Global Times*, 16 August 2018, https://bit.ly/2PpPTHT
5. 'Powering the Belt and Road', Mercator Institute of China Studies (MERICS), 27 June 2019, https://bit.ly/32bogon

Chapter 7: Trading and Slipping

1. Sutirtho Patranobis, 'Trade between India and China to cross $100 billion, says envoy Vikram Misri', *Hindustan Times*, 6 June 2019, https://bit.ly/2zxd5ZU
2. 'China opens door to Indian generics', China Policy, 24 June 2019.
3. 'Revised law opens the doors to cheap generic Indian medicines', *Global Times*, 28 August 2019.
4. 'Opinion: China Must Wake Up to Injustice of High Drug Prices', Caixin, 5 July 2018.

Chapter 8: Public Discourses: A Crucial Challenge

1. David Bandurski, 'China, rhetorical giant?', China Media Project, 24 June 2017, https://bit.ly/2PsZkpV
2. 'PLA holds drills amid Doklam tensions', *Global Times*, 20 August 2017, https://bit.ly/2Zt6O0E
3. Yoichi Funabashi, 'Toward a free and open Indo-Pacific', the *Japan Times*, 10 May 2018, https://bit.ly/32c5qfO

Chapter 11: The Trump Effects

1. Colin Lecher, 'White House cracks down on Huawei equipment sales with executive order', the *Verge*, 15 May 2019, https://bit.ly/2W0xrHX
2. Xie Yu, 'Vietnam and India see explosion in direct investment from China as tech suppliers shift production overseas, says Goldman Sachs', *South China Morning Post*, 24 June 2019.

3. Spencer Kimball, 'Trump says tariffs on $200 billions of Chinese goods will increase to 25%', CNBC, 5 May 2019, https://cnb.cx/2DQ1kjM
4. Saibal Dasgupta, 'China Prepares for Trade Talks despite Trump's New Threat', VOA News, 6 May 2019, https://bit.ly/2zvDPd9
5. Ken Bredemeier, 'China Imposes Tariffs on $60 Billion in US Exports', VOA News, 13 May 2019, https://bit.ly/30MqCZo
6. Saibal Dasgupta, 'In Trade War, How Much Can Beijing Fight Back?', VOA News, 17 May 2019, https://bit.ly/2NSESwr
7. ———, 'Analysts: Potential Trade Deal Tough Challenge for China's Communist Party Leaders', VOA News, 10 April 2019, https://bit.ly/2UpJtXZ.
8. Ibid.
9. ———, 'Alibaba Chief's Next Move May Reveal a Chinese Game Plan', VOA News, 18 September 2018, https://bit.ly/2ZBkPIY
10. Ibid.
11. ———, 'US rejects Tesla bid for tariff exemption for autopilot brain', Reuters, 4 May 2019.
12. 'China Manufacturing 2025: Putting Industrial Policy Ahead of Market Forces', European Chamber of Commerce in China, 23 July 2019, https://bit.ly/2HiaMi0
13. 'Man and Machines in Industry 4.0', Boston Consulting Group, 28 September 2015, https://on.bcg.com/30HATpQ
14. 'China Manufacturing 2025: Putting Industrial Policy Ahead of Market Forces', European Chamber of Commerce in China, 23 July 2019